PHILOSOPHICAL PERSPECTIVES
ON PUNISHMENT

Publication Number 697

AMERICAN LECTURE SERIES®

A Monograph in

The BANNERSTONE DIVISION *of*
AMERICAN LECTURES IN PHILOSOPHY

Edited by

MARVIN FARBER

State University of New York at Buffalo

PHILOSOPHICAL PERSPECTIVES ON PUNISHMENT

Compiled and Edited by

EDWARD H. MADDEN

State University of New York at Buffalo

ROLLO HANDY

State University of New York at Buffalo

and

MARVIN FARBER

State University of New York at Buffalo

CHARLES C THOMAS • PUBLISHER

Springfield • Illinois • U.S.A.

Published and Distributed Throughout the World by

CHARLES C THOMAS • PUBLISHER

BANNERSTONE HOUSE

301-327 East Lawrence Avenue, Springfield, Illinois, U.S.A.

NATCHEZ PLANTATION HOUSE

735 North Atlantic Boulevard, Fort Lauderdale, Florida, U.S.A.

With THOMAS BOOKS *careful attention is given to all details of
manufacturing and design. It is the Publisher's desire to present books
that are satisfactory as to their physical qualities and artistic possibilities
and appropriate for their particular use.* THOMAS BOOKS *will be true
to those laws of quality that assure a good name and good will.*

CONTRIBUTORS

Charles A. Baylis
Duke University
Durham, North Carolina

Brand Blanshard
Yale University
New Haven, Connecticut

C. J. Ducasse
Brown University
Providence, Rhode Island

Berkley B. Eddins
State University of New York at Buffalo

Mitchell Franklin
Law School
Tulane University
New Orleans, Louisiana

Llewellyn Gross
State University of New York at Buffalo

P. H. Hare
State University of New York at Buffalo

J. D. Hyman
State University of New York at Buffalo

Richard A. Koehl
State University of New York at Buffalo

Marvin K. Opler
State University of New York at Buffalo

J. R. Pratt
State University of New York at Buffalo

Peter F. Regan
State University of New York at Buffalo

v

PREFACE

A CCORDING TO BRAND BLANSHARD ". . . punishment is unpleasant to inflict and not particularly pleasant to discuss. But
we clearly need to discuss it." Such discussion is important for
at least two reasons. On the one hand, a careful analysis of the
notion of punishment yields insight into the many practical problems of penology and, on the other, leads to the basic problems
of ethical theory, including the perennially fascinating problems
at issue between teleologists and deontologists. How one decides
the issues of punishment and other problems of a similar type-
level, in fact, usually decides what one's ultimate moral commitment will be. Only those who are either sanguine or dogmatic
commit themselves on the primary issues first and then inexorably
unfold the consequences, whatever they may be, for moral concerns on the type-level of punishment and penology. In ethics,
as elsewhere in philosophy, one should reach first principles at
the end of inquiry.

This book comprises the four major addresses, eight commentaries, and four replies to comments, all of which were read at the
symposium on Philosophical Perspectives on Punishment held at
the State University of New York at Buffalo on Friday, October
7, 1966. The four major addresses were delivered by Professors
Charles A. Baylis, Brand Blanshard, C. J. Ducasse, and Mitchell
Franklin. The aim of the symposium was to consider in detail,
and from a variety of perspectives, an important philosophical
problem of great interest for scholars in related disciplines. Three
of the major papers were written by philosophers, and the fourth
by a legal scholar. Commentaries were read by participants from
philosophy, law, sociology, psychiatry, and anthropology.

The papers by Professors Baylis, Blanshard, and Ducasse were
devoted to critical and analytical inquiries into various philosophical justifications of punishment. Professor Franklin's historical paper focused on the contribution of several legal scholars

and philosophers to the development of a general theory of criminal responsibility. In view of the marked differences in the general interests and systematic views of the three philosophers, the convergence in certain crucial respects of their views on punishment is remarkable. They are at one in rejecting retributivist and deontological views of punishment, although the latter view is not wholly without some support in this volume. Professor Franklin's paper, with its historical focus, should be of special interest to Hegel scholars and to existentialists. Considering that all four papers were written completely independently of each other, the number of common themes discussed is worthy of note.

The symposium committee members, editors of this volume, are deeply grateful to the College of Arts and Sciences, State University of New York at Buffalo, for providing funds for this discussion of punishment and to the Charles C Thomas Company for prompt publication of the proceedings. We are also obliged to William Baumer, John Kearns, Charles Lambros, and Thomas Perry for being chairmen of the sessions and to George Benedict, Peter Hare, Marian Madden, J. R. Pratt, Ronald Stein, and Jane Warren for help in arranging the numerous details of the symposium and for assistance in preparing the manuscript for publication. To the main speakers, the commentators, and the chairmen we are, of course, grateful, obliged, and more, for their excellent efforts.

EDWARD H. MADDEN
ROLLO HANDY
MARVIN FARBER
Buffalo, New York

CONTENTS

ix

PHILOSOPHICAL PERSPECTIVES
ON PUNISHMENT

The following books have appeared thus far in this Series:

I

PHILOSOPHY AND WISDOM IN PUNISHMENT AND REWARD

C. J. Ducasse

A PHILOSOPHICAL DISCUSSION of the question as to when punishment is or is not wise should, I believe, consider also to some extent the parallel although less tormenting question concerning the opposite of punishment, namely: reward. In this address I shall therefore feel free to touch at some points also on the latter.

Inasmuch, however, as the word *philosophy* is the first in the title of my address, I must begin with a summary statement of what I conceive philosophy essentially to be; of the kind of practical utility it has; and of the method it must employ if it is to progress toward its aims.

Philosophy and Wisdom

The Greek verb, *philosophein,* is first used by Herodotus. It occurs in his account of a conversation between Solon and King Croesus, in the course of which the king says to Solon: "I have heard that thou *philosopheon* (philosophizing) hast travelled over many lands for the purpose of observing."[1]

There is, however, also a tradition that Pythagoras had been the first to employ the word *philosophy* and to refer to himself as a philosopher. But very little is really known of Pythagoras personally, and this tradition appears to have ". . . hardly any claim to be regarded as authentic."[2]

Use of the term *philosophy* to mean the seeking of knowledge did not become popular during the next two centuries. The men who strove to gain knowledge referred to themselves not as lovers of wisdom (philosophers), but as wise men (sophoi). Socrates derided the latter appellation and described himself more

3

modestly as a philosopher—a lover and seeker of wisdom. But no distinction was made between wisdom and knowledge.

I conceive philosophy to be essentially *the love and pursuit of the kinds of knowledge necessary for wisdom* and, ideally, also sufficient for it. The first task which my conception of the method fertile in the pursuit of wisdom assigns to a metaphilosopher—that is to a philosopher attempting, as I am now doing, to formulate a philosophy of philosophy—is to state as precisely as possible what is meant by wisdom. What is meant, for example, when one speaks of the wisdom or folly of a particular course of action, or of the decision to embark on that course; or, more specifically, of the wisdom or folly of punishing, or of rewarding, or of treating in some manner different from either of these, a particular living being who has done a certain thing?

The answer to this question, I now submit, is that *wisdom consists in knowledge of what, in given circumstances, would on the whole be the best thing which a person having a given equipment could do.*[3]

Scientific Method in Philosophy

Wisdom consists, thus, not in irresponsible opinion but in *knowledge,* properly so called (concerning what the rest of that definition specifies), and entails that the pursuit of wisdom is by intent a *scientific* pursuit. The adjective *scientific,* as applied to inquiry, means *knowledge-yielding* inquiry even when, as often in the natural sciences too, the knowledge obtained is knowledge only of probabilities. That knowledge is what philosophers seek concerning the philosophical questions they ask, is automatically testified to whenever the grounds they offer for the assertions they make or against some of those made by their opponents are epistemic or logical, not fideistic, aesthetic, or other epistemically irrelevant grounds.

In each science, however, the general principles of scientific method take some special forms dictated by the distinctive subject matter of the particular science concerned. In philosophy, the fundamental special form which scientific method must take (if philosophy is not to go on forever discussing the same problems without solving them) is to define as precisely as possible, but in a nonarbitrary manner, the terms on whose meaning depends the answer to the particular question in the formulation of which they are employed and where they are, therefore, "key" terms.

That a definition is nonarbitrary in this instance means it is substitutable for the term defined without thereby altering the truth-values or the logical implications of various statements where the term occurs that illustrate the term's particular usage with which one is concerned. The definition is, then, an *induction* from a representative sample of that usage. The term whose definition is so obtained then becomes a technical term. That is, it becomes an instrument of precision for the detection of implications latent in that usage, but not discernible so long as one's understanding of the term's meaning is only the habit-begotten, but unanalyzed understanding one has of it as employed in stereotyped phrases. Philosophy conceived as a science can no more do without technical terms as just now defined than can the other sciences.[4]

Four Tasks Necessary to Make Wise Decisions

My definition of the term wisdom offered in what precedes combines four different tasks which a person (P) must perform if his decision, regardless as to what, is to be wise; for instance, his decision, in a given concrete case, as to whether punishing, or rewarding, or some other course of action would be wise.

First, he should inform himself as accurately and completely as possible of the empirical facts in the particular case. If, for example, the person who in a specific case has committed a crime was not normally rational but neurotic or psychotic, this fact would obviously be relevant in attempting to decide whether punishing him would be wise (or perhaps even really possible).

Second, P should take stock of the diverse means available in the case, employment of any one of which would achieve a particular end; he should also take stock of the diverse ends which could be achieved in the case with the available means.

Third, P should consider the values—positive and negative, intrinsic and instrumental—which would be generated by each of the courses of action found possible in the case.

Fourth, then, P should finally judge which of those courses of action would on the whole be best or, as the case might be, least bad. That is, which would probably generate more positive value and/or less negative value for the persons it affected than any of the alternative possible courses of action.

Needless to say, judgment as to these respective probabilities would in most cases be difficult, and therefore far from confident. Nevertheless, it would be the wisest made possible by the circumstances of the case and *P's* information, plus his axiological judgment.

Current Discussions of Punishment

I have now set forth what I conceive philosophy essentially to be, what constitutes its far-reaching, practical importance, and what specific form the knowledge-yielding method has to take in philosophy. I shall, in the sequel, consider various crucial questions concerning punishment and reward for which responsible answers become discernible when philosophical inquiry is carried on in accordance with the method described.

First, however, permit me to make a few words of comment concerning the current discussions of punishment considered by Professor Donald Loftsgordon in a valuable article entitled "Present-day British Philosophers on Punishment" *(Journal of Philosophy,* June 9, 1966). My reason for calling attention to that article at this point is that, so far at least as may be gathered from its contents, the British philosophers cited in it seem to assume that punishment is always *of* some human being *by* some human agent or agency; also, that punishment is inherently always for violation of some moral or legal rule.

These two assumptions, however, would gratuitously limit greatly the applicability of the term *punishment,* for there is such a thing as punishment of an animal by a human being: for instance, my having slapped my dear Siamese cat when I saw him sharpening his claws on the upholstery of a chair. Also, there is such a thing as punishment of an animal by another animal, such as a mother cat's scratching a naïve dog who was approaching her kittens. There is also punishment of a human being by an animal, as in a dog's growling readiness to bite me when I approached the kittens he had come to love.

Moreover, anyone—be it a tyrant, a despot, or dictator, or the owner of a slave or of an animal—who for the time being has autocratic power over certain sentient beings can, simply by virtue of having such power, punish or reward one of them for having done something the autocratic ruler happened to dislike, (or like) but which was neither immoral nor specifically moral, and was neither a violation of, nor a compliance with, any rule of conduct the ruler had yet promulgated.

The realm of congruous applicability of the term *punishment* (and, *mutatis mutandis,* of the term *reward)* therefore, is substantially wider than it would be made by the five characteristics Loftsgordon quotes, which Antony Flew offered all together as defining punishment.

The Definition of Punishment

In the outline of the philosophy of punishment to be offered in the remainder of my paper, I shall proceed by considering in turn the chief questions relating to punishment which arise in the light of a really comprehensive definition of the term. Then, (in accordance with the conception of scientific method in philosophy described earlier) I shall continue by offering definitions— attemptedly both precise and nonarbitrary—of the terms employed in those questions that are "key" terms in the sense that the answers to the questions turn on the meaning of those terms.

The first question is, of course, what precisely does *punishing* mean? And here it is crucial to notice that punishing, and hence punishment, too, has at least two senses. In one of them, (of which the definition submitted later offers an analysis) punishment is inherently of a *sentient* being, and *for,* i.e., because of, its doing or having done "something wrong." But in the other sense, punishment is not necessarily of, or by, a sentient being; and is not because of its undergoer's doing or having done any wrong. An example of the use of the term in this sense would be: "Hurricane *Inez* severely punished the crops and the coasts of Cuba and of other Caribbean regions." In this and other examples of punishing used in the second of its two senses, *to punish* means simply *to cause damage, destruction, or hardship* to what undergoes it, which need not, but can be, a sentient being.

The definition now about to be submitted is of punishment in the first of the two senses distinguished: i.e., in the sense the term has when employed in such phrases as: punishment for theft; punishment for murder; for insolence; for perjury, or "wrongdoing" of some other kind. That particular definition, including its motivation, is as follows:

> *Punishment means purposive infliction of pain, loss, suffering, deprivation, or other hardship on the undergoer; such hardship being inflicted because the undergoer is known by the de facto ruler to be doing, or to have done, some particular thing the latter disapproves. The immediate purpose of inflicting the hardship is to cause the wrongdoer to desist from his present wrongdoing, and/or to deter him from repeating in the future the disapproved thing he is known to be doing or to have done.*

The parties figuring in punishment thus are:
1. The undergoer *(U)* of it
2. The at the time *de facto* ruler *(R)* who decides that punishment is to be inflicted on *U*
3. The inflicter *(I)* of it, who may be *R* himself or an agent of his
4. If the infliction of hardship on *U* is public or is published, and the wrongdoing for which hardship is being inflicted on *U* is likewise public or published, then those *members of the public* who come to know both of these become automatically one of the parties concerned; for this knowledge may deter their yielding to a possible temptation to do something like the same kind of wrong themselves.

In connection with the definition of punishment I have given, it should be pointed out that what the *R* actually does to *U* may not really constitute punishment as defined. If *R* only believes but does not really know that what he does to the wrongdoer is ranked as hardship by the latter, then *R* has not in fact punished *U* but only *believes* he has. An interesting illustration of this, called to my attention by Roderick Chisholm, is that of destitute people in Chicago and New York who commit a minor nuisance in order to be arrested and "punished'" by being given a place to sleep for the night: a cell in jail, and something to eat. After all, going to jail is one way of making a living!

The Purposiveness of Punishment

The definition of punishment specifies that punishing is an inherently *purposive* activity. Purposive activity, however, may be either *autotelic or heterotelic;* that is, performed either for its own sake, or for the sake of some effect which the activity causes. But autotelic infliction of an experience ranked as hardship by the undergoer of it is, *qua autotelic,* not punitive but either sadistic or masochistic, depending on whether the undergoer is other than the inflicter, or is the inflicter himself. Hence activity purposely causative of an experience disliked by the undergoer of it can be punishment *only if* (but is not necessarily punishment *if)* that activity is heterotelic.

An example making this evident would be that of a dentist who grinds out a cavity in a patient's tooth. His activity in so doing is purposive, and is also disagreeable to the patient; but the dentist's purpose in grinding the tooth is not to punish the patient for something the latter has done or failed to do; nor is it to grind the tooth sadistically just because the grinding is disagreeable to the patient. The dentist's purpose is simply to make the cavity ready for filling.

On the other hand, his grinding a cavity that needs filling *could* be punishment only if the patient—perhaps the dentist's own child—had been ordered in the past to brush his teeth regularly but had not bothered to do so. The grinding would then be punishment, but only in so far as the dentist, having reminded the patient of the order he had been given but had disobeyed, then did, for emphasis, but tacitly, make the grinding more disagreeable than it would have needed to be simply to get the cavity ready for filling.

Purposive Activity As Differentiated from Mechanical

The next thing we need to be quite clear about is what differentiates *telic,* i.e., purposive activity in general—irrespective of whether it be specifically autotelic or heterotelic—from *atelic,* i.e., mechanical activity, no matter whether the latter be physical or mental.

The answer, I submit, is that in purposive activity the proximate *(vs.* mediated) cause of the activity consists, either wholly or in part, of a *conation,* a *craving;* whereas in mechanical activity its proximate cause does not consist either wholly or in part of a conation.

A conation, however, may be either blind or cognizant; that is, either unaccompanied, or accompanied, by awareness of its conatum; i.e., of what would satisfy the conation. For instance, the conation which causes a neonate's crying is not cognizant but blind: It occurs without awareness in the neonate that milk is what he craves.

On the other hand, what then is called *desire* consists in conation cognizant of what would satisfy it. But here it is important to notice that the activity which a desire generates may be either heuristic activity (trial-and-error, i.e., exploratory search for some way of causing fulfillment of one's desire); or skillful activity (i.e., dexterous, "know-how" activity); or instructed activity (i.e., activity guided by a recipe, by directions as to how to proceed).[5]

Characteristics Which Capacitate an Entity to Act Punitively

In the light provided by the distinctions already made (a) between purposive and mechanical activity, (b) between blind and cognizant purposive activity, and (c) between cognizant purposive activity which is exploratory, skilled, or informed, we are now in position to specify characteristics necessary and together sufficient to capacitate an entity to act punitively. We can also, correspondingly, specify the characteristics necessary and jointly sufficient to capacitate an entity to undergo punishment. This will enable us then to mention some of the kinds of entities which less obviously have, or lack, one or the other of these capacities.

The following characteristics qualify an entity to act punitively: (a) It must have power to inflict on some entity capable of being punished an experience disliked by the latter. (b) It must be capable of purposive activity, not blind (like the neonate's) but cognizant of what it aims to accomplish.

Evidently, not only most human beings but also certain animals have these characteristics. An example cited earlier as obvious even prior to analysis was that of a mother cat who scratched a dog approaching her kittens. Of course, what the cat was going to do was not known by her conceptually. Nor was it known by her merely behaviorally; that is, she experienced a conation not only to make certain movements, but to scratch the dog; just as, when any one of us sees a ball about to hit his face, he feels impelled not just to move his hand up, but to stop the ball with his hand.

Another example, in which the animal is an insect, would be that of a hornet which stings a man who disturbs his nest or approaches it too closely. The hornet aims to sting the man, just as the man who sees the hornet about to sting him then aims to swat the hornet.

On the other hand, here is an example in which the "death penalty" would not really be penalty, i.e., not punishment. Suppose a man is accused of a crime for which the death penalty is mandatory. Suppose the jury, having heard the evidence, concludes, late one evening while the accused is asleep in jail, that he is guilty. Then, if carbon monoxide were piped into his jail cell, this, without awakening him, would cause him to die. Since the dislike which characterizes the process of dying when it is conscious would not be experienced by the man asleep in jail, killing him in this manner would not constitute punishment.

Characteristics Without Which
an Entity Is Not Capable of Being Punished

The characteristics necessary and together sufficient to make an entity capable of being punished are as follows:

1. The entity must be a conscious being
2. It must be capable of experiences it dislikes
3. It must be "guilty," i.e., be doing or have done something disapproved, i.e., held to be "wrong," by R who *de facto* has power to make the entity undergo experiences it dislikes
4. The entity must be such that infliction upon it of experiences it dislikes (if the infliction is wise in timing, in frequency, in kind, and in degree of severity) causes the entity *to stop* such present wrongdoing, and deters the entity to some extent from repeating it in the future.

The fact that punishment is intended by R to deter U from repeating in the future the particular wrongdoing for which he is now being punished implies that not human beings alone, and not all human beings, but *all and none but* beings capable of such conditioning, can be treated in a manner properly called punishment. These beings would include not only normal human beings, but also normal domestic animals; also, such lower animals, including many insects, as are capable of being "taught" by a disliked experience attendant on behavior of a particularly wrong type, not to behave again in that wrong manner. Hence if, as I read recently somewhere, it is true that the housefly is not capable of such conditioning, then *ex vi termini,* it is impossible to punish a housefly. What remains possible is only to shoo it away, or to kill it, or to catch it and release it outdoors.

The Retributivist Contention That Punishment of the Guilty Is Morally Good Because It Is Just

Loftsgordon, in the article cited earlier, refers to Armstrong's contention that the utilitarian conception of what morally justifies punishment is not the only logically possible one. He quotes what Armstrong (*Mind,* October 1961, p. 483) offers as a ". . . possible, though perhaps poor . . ." retributivist account of what morally justifies punishment. Armstrong's statement itself reads: "The moral justification of punishment is simply that the infliction of pain on those who have inflicted pain on others is a Good-in-itself, since it is a species of justice."

The fact I have stressed, however, that not only a human being but an animal, too, can be punished by a human being, provides a revealing perspective on what a retributivist justification of punishment would permit. If *some degree of deterrence* from repeating the wrongdoing for which punishment is inflicted is not necessary to make punishment morally just, then it would be morally just, for instance, to lash a dog today because he bit the postman ten days ago. Doing so, of course, would not teach the dog anything, since he would not know why he is being lashed. But if retribution is morally just anyway, lashing the dog today would be *just* if the pain inflicted on the dog is equal to the pain he inflicted on the postman ten days ago. Indeed, if instead of lashing the dog one were to bite his leg, this would be even more *just,* i.e., be more nearly *just the same as,* what he did to the postman!

But whether it would thus be not merely quantitatively just, but also morally just in a sense more relevant than that merely quantitative one, is the crucial question. And it seems to me evident that lashing the dog today for having bitten the postman ten days ago would be morally unjust and constitute purely gratuitous and therefore stupid cruelty, since it would accomplish nothing in protecting the postman from being bitten again by the dog.

The retributivist conception of morally just punishment is essentially the same as that set forth in the Old Testament (Lev. 24:17) where we read: ". . . he who kills a man shall surely be put to death"; also: ". . . if a man causes a disfigurement in his neighbor, [then] as he has done, so shall it be done to him; fracture for fracture, eye for eye, tooth for tooth. . . ." (Lev. 24: 19, 20.)

That this is but a codification of an automatic impulse to angry reaction when one is injured or frustrated becomes even more evident when one adverts to the fact, called to my attention by my colleague Roderick Chisholm, that one occasionally reacts in similar manner when the entity whose behavior angers one is not a sentient being but a wholly physical mechanism; for instance a clock or an engine whose failing to function when it should causes one to smash or kick it angrily.

It seems to me obvious that in cases where the wisdom or folly of punishment is in question, a precept more truly moral than the retributivist ". . . eye for an eye, a tooth for a tooth . . ." is the humanitarian precept laid down by Jesus, to do unto others as one would have them do to oneself; or, in the words of the gospel according to Matthew 7:12: "So whatever you wish that men would do to you, do so to them . . ."; and in the gospel according to Luke 6:31: "As you wish that men would do to you, do so to them." (Holy Bible, Revised Standard Version.)

However, leaving now aside both the retributivist and the humanitarian biblical injunctions I have just quoted, I would like to ask the retributivist what, according to his conception of the morality of punishment, ought to be done in the following highly hypothetical case. Suppose one of these days pharmacologists were to compound a pill the swallowing of which would immediately and permanently turn even the most vicious of criminals into a saint. Ought the criminal then be made to swallow the pill, instead of being punished? Or ought he to be punished anyway, since he "deserves" it, and not be given the pill? Or ought he first to be punished since he "deserves" it, so that "justice" be done, and only afterwards be made to swallow the pill?

The Sound As Well As Erroneous Factors in the Deontological Contention That the Morality or Immorality of an Act Is Known Intuitively

As regards now this deontological contention, I submit that what is sound in it is that, in certain concrete individual cases, we are intuitively so completely confident of the morality or immorality of the particular act in the case concerned that we are ready to offer it as a defining instance of what we mean by a "moral" or by an "immoral" act.

On the other hand, generalizations we make almost automatically on the basis of our intuition in a concrete case offered by us as such a defining instance are unsound; patently valid exceptions to them are always imaginable. The best way to make this evident briefly is in terms of some specific concrete act and its concrete circumstances. Let us take as an example the historical case of Nero's killing his mother.

I would offer it as a defining instance—a paradigm case—of what I mean by a "morally wrong" act. When a person *(P)* however, who likewise so regards it, passes from the declaration that that individual, concrete, historical act was morally wrong, to the generalization, "Matricide is morally wrong," his latter statement automatically formulates three things together. One is *P's* intuitive disapproval of Nero's historical act; another is *P's* reason for disapproving it, namely, that the act has the features which the word *matricide* describes; and third is *P's* commitment to disapprove any other act resembling Nero's.

But the generalization, "Matricide is morally wrong," abstracts illegitimately from certain of the concrete and essential features of Nero's act. Suppose, for example, that *P's* own mother, whom he loved dearly, somehow came to be regarded as a witch in the days when ecclesiastical authorities could and did act in accordance with the Biblical commandment: "You shall not permit a sorceress to live" (Exod. 22:18). Suppose she had therefore been condemned to be burned alive; that she then entreated her son to spare her this torture by plunging a quick knife into her heart, and that, out of love and compassion, he did so, at the cost of his own life. The possibility of such a case, where I submit that matricide would be morally right and indeed noble, makes evident that the unqualified generalization, "Matricide is morally wrong," is unwarrantedly sweeping.

Thus, the fact which ultimately makes clear both what is sound and what is erroneous in the deontologist's contention that the morality or immorality of items of conduct is known intuitively is that, on one hand, there are many cases where *P* has no doubt at all that a certain concrete act which he witnessed or otherwise came to have knowledge of, was moral or, as the case may be, immoral, i.e., ought or ought not to have been done. On the other hand, there are many situations where *P* has no such clear and confident *pro* or *contra* intuition concerning a particular form of conduct enacted or contemplated by him or by another person; but where, instead *P is in doubt and hesitates.* These are the cases where he needs some principle or criterion (which deontological ethics does not provide whereas utilitarianism does) from which to deduce whether the conduct in view is, more probably than not, morally right, or as the case may be, morally wrong.[6]

Concerning the fact I have stressed, that there are concrete cases of conduct which, intuitively, we are ready to offer as defining instances of what we mean by "moral" or by "immoral" conduct, it should now be added that we might eventually come to deny some of them that status. But this would occur only if we had then noticed in the particular concrete case concerned, some overlooked feature of such importance that when we consider it in addition to the others, we then see clearly why that concrete case, after all, does not rank as a defining instance of what we mean by a "moral," or as the case may be, an "immoral" act.

Cases Where Imposition of Hardship Is Truly Punishment: Its Justifiability As an Indispensable Psychological Deterrent

Imposition of hardship on the wrongdoer is justified in certain cases because it is psychologically indispensable and deters the particular wrongdoer from repeating his wrongdoing—this even when the wrongdoing is not only involuntary, but is in itself highly distressing to the wrongdoer. In such cases, of course, the imposition of hardship truly is punishment.

A case recently publicized widely illustrating this particular situation is that of a girl who for 154 days sneezed many times each day, the number of such sneezes being decreased only somewhat by hypnotic and other treatment as was employed. What finally brought her compulsive sneezing to an end, however, was the attaching of electrodes to the girl's arms, and the hanging of a microphone around her neck, which, when she sneezed, triggered a device sending a mildly punishing electric shock through her arms. When this treatment began, she was sneezing every 40 seconds. In the first 30 minutes of the treatment, she sneezed only 22 times, and in the next 30 minutes only 12 times. By the time this electric shock treatment had lasted 2 hours and 20 minutes, she was cured.

The psychological principle at work, of course, is the same as that implicit in the fact that touching a hot stove and getting at once painfully burned causes one automatically to refrain from touching hot stoves again. If pickpockets were similarly painfully burned or cut by the purse they reach for, they would similarly stop picking pockets (or at least, stop doing it with their bare hands!). Punishment and reward are widely and effectively employed in laboratories and in the training of domestic animals. They can be equally effective with children and adults, provided, as already mentioned, that the punishment or reward is intelligent in timing, in kind, in magnitude, and in frequency.

Cases Where Imposition of Hardship for Wrongdoing Is Psychologically Unjustified Because It Is Psychologically Impotent to Deter

In cases where imposition of hardship on a wrongdoer for something he has done is psychologically impotent to deter him to some extent from repeating his wrongdoing, such imposition does not constitute punishment. Yet, imposition of certain forms of hardship on the wrongdoer (such as imprisonment, or confinement in an asylum for the mentally defective) may even then be justified in *physically* preventing the wrongdoer from repeating his wrongdoing and, consequently, in protecting society from the harm which repetition of his wrongdoing would do.

If, however, as I understand is the fact, more than two-thirds of the convicts in our penitentiaries or houses of correction are repeaters, then the hardship of imprisonment imposed on them is thereby shown to have been psychologically impotent to deter them from repeating their wrongdoing; therefore, *ex vi termini,* not really to have constituted punishment, although that had been the intention and belief at the time. Indeed, the hardship which the imposed imprisonment constituted, and in addition the sometimes stupid or deliberately brutal treatment of the prisoners, is likely to have generated in those of them who later repeated their wrongdoing a grudge that made even more probable the repetition of their wrongdoing when liberated after having served their sentence.

This naturally raises the question as to the nature of the reforms in the prison system now extant. Such reforms are imperative if prisons are to perform, more effectively than they now do, the function which they are intended ultimately to perform, and which would most rationally justify their existence: the protection of society from repetitions of the wrongdoings of criminals.

The most interesting, intimately informed, and rational discussion of this question I have seen was written by a highly intelligent ex-convict, Hal Hollister, on parole from a life sentence after thirteen years served in a state penitentiary. It was published in *Harper's Magazine,* (August 1962) under the title, "An Ex-convict's Scheme for Practical Prisons." He rightly assumes that ". . . the one overall goal [of a prison system] that makes sense" is to protect society. But the clerical work he had to do in the prison, his editing for seven years the prison's monthly inmate magazine, and his teaching for two years in the prison school—all gave him intimate, solid knowledge of the great diversity of psychological make-ups among his fellow prisoners. This knowledge now enables him to approach in an intelligently realistic manner an attempt to outline a more practical plan for prisons. He suggests not treating alike prisoners psychologically incapable of reformation and prisoners capable of more or less gradual reformation if treated in a manner appropriate to their individual psychological constitutions, as well as those who are what he aptly calls "accidental or circumstantial criminals."

An interview with Myrl E. Alexander, Director of the Bureau of Prisons, United States Department of Justice, published in *U. S. News and World Report* (July 11, 1966) indicates that an intelligently realistic ". . . revolution in the treatment of criminals . . ." is under way in this country.

One of the devices found effective with certain of the convicts is the "work furlough" idea employed now for some eight years in Santa Clara County, in California. It is described in *The New York Times Magazine* (November 14, 1965) in an article by Gertrude Samuels entitled, "Working Their Way Through Jail." It allows selected prisoners to leave the jail daily, in the morning, to work at standard wages at a job in the community until 4:30 P.M., when they must return to jail until the next morning. This arrangement enables a prisoner to support his family during the time of his sentence, to pay his fine, or to take care of other expenses. The article states that the basic objective of the plan is ". . . to build a bridge of self-respect and responsibility, between abnormal prison life and normal commmunity living."

To prevent repetition of crimes and thus protect society is, of course, highly important. But as Bertrand Russell states in the passage quoted by Loftsgordon in his article, the problem of doing this ". . . should be treated in a purely scientific spirit." Actually this means with no more suffering to the criminal than may be necessary, as well as sufficient, to cure his criminal tendencies.

References

1. *Herodotus* I-30. This translation of the passage is given in Ueberweg's *History of Philosophy* as translated into English (New York, Scribner, 1898, vol. 1, p. 2) where mention is also made that in *Herodotus* I-50 *philosophia* is used, the knowledge referred to there being knowledge of the stars. The passage from *Herodotus* I-30 is translated more fully by A. D. Godley in his *Herodotus* as follows: "We have heard much of you, by reason of your wisdom and your wanderings, how that you have travelled far to seek knowledge [philosopheon] and to see the world. . . ."
2. PATTISON, A. S. P.: Philosophy. *Encycl Britannica,* 11th ed., vol. 21, p. 440.

3. This is the definition I offered some years ago in an address to the Phi Beta Kappa Society entitled: The guide of life. *The KEY Reporter, 24,* 1958.

4. DUCASSE, C. J.: Philosophy can become a science. *Revue Int de Philosophie,* No. 47, Fasc. 1, 1959. In this article, a much more detailed statement and illustration is given than there is room for here, of the form which scientific method has to take in philosophy.

5. DUCASSE, C. J.: Life, telism, and mechanism. *Philosophy and Phenomenological Research, 20,* 1959. A more complete exposition than there is room for here of the essential difference between purposiveness and mechanism (including servo-mechanism) is provided in this paper presented at the Second Plenary Session of the 1957 Interamerican Congress of Philosophy. Substantially the same analysis of the several levels of purposiveness was later incorporated in sections 3 to 10 of Chapter XI of the writer's *The Belief in a Life after Death.* Springfield, Thomas, 1961.

6. DUCASSE, C. J.: Scientific method in ethics. *Philosophy and Phenomenological Research, 14,* 1953.

   DUCASSE, C. J.: Concerning the logical status of criteria of morality. *Philosophy and Phenomenological Research, 23,* 1962.

PROFESSOR DUCASSE AND THE MEANING OF "PUNISHMENT"

J. R. PRATT

Professor Ducasse conceives philosophy to be "the love and pursuit of the kinds of knowledge . . . of what, in given circumstances, would on the whole be the best thing which a person having a given equipment could do." The *way* philosophy pursues such knowledge is by constructing definitions; philosophy must, he says:

> . . . define as precisely as possible, but in a nonarbitrary manner, the terms on whose meaning depends the answer to the particular question in the formulation of which they are employed and where they are, therefore, 'key' terms.

I contend that either Professor Ducasse's definition of *punishment* is extremely arbitrary, or else he misdescribes the way he has acquired the kind of knowledge philosophy lovingly pursues.

To focus attention on my purpose, let me quote Professor Ducasse's statement as to what a definition must be to be *non*arbitrary:

> . . . that a definition is *nonarbitrary* . . . means it is substitutable for the term defined without thereby altering the truth-values or the logical implications of various statements where the term occurs that illustrate the term's particular usage with which one is concerned, The definition is, then, an *induction* from a representative sample of that usage. . . .

Given Professor Ducasse's conception of philosophy, discussion of his definition of *punishment* must be against the backdrop of a recognition of what practical problems the definition he offers is intended to solve. As I interpret the point of the last sections of his address, he is concerned about answering the following question: "What, in modern-day circumstances in our society, would, on the whole, be the wisest way to punish those who break the laws of our society, given the means available to us?" It is in answer to such questions that philosophers are supposed to pursue knowledge by defining the key terms of the questions they confront. The answer Professor Ducasse gives is that punishment should involve ". . . no more suffering to the criminal than may be necessary, as well as sufficient, to cure his criminal tendencies."

My claim is that this answer, laudable though it be, is not evolved from a nonarbitrary definition of *punishment*. One simply cannot arrive at a definition which will say what *wise* punishment is by induction from a representative sample of the usage of the term "punishment." This particular usage reveals that certain things are called punishments when they are patently unwise, unjust, and immoral. Only if people invariably punished wisely and referred only to such wise punishments as punishments could one expect to find out what wise punishment is by a definition based on representative samples from usage.

In short, I submit that Professor Ducasse cannot be defining *punishment* in the way he says he is—inductively from representative samples from usage—and simultaneously be arriving at a resolution of what constitutes wise punishment on the basis of that definition.

So, I shall force this point by presenting a number of counter-examples which establish that as an induction from representative samples, Professor Ducasse's definition of *punishment* both *excludes* things that usage accounts as cases of punishment and *includes* things that usage refuses to account as cases of punishment. What I hope to achieve is this: I hope to direct discussion away from the definition of terms, "key" or otherwise, toward the justification and defense of what punishment *should* be. Indeed, as I interpret him, Professor Ducasse espouses a particular theory of punishment, one which is actually a weak version of the deterrence theory. So, some of my counter-examples are chosen not only to establish the arbitrariness of his definition as the type he maintains it is, but also to establish that his theory of punishment is inadequate when one turns to questions of justification.

Compressed, Professor Ducasse's definition is this: R stands for "*de facto* ruler"; U, undergoer of punishment; A, act or state of affairs constituting punishment; D, the deed U is alleged to be doing or to have done.

R punishes U by bringing about A if and only if:

1. A is the purposive infliction of some hardship on U
2. R brings about A because R knows that U is "guilty" of doing or having done D
3. The immediate purpose of bringing about A is

(a) to cause U to desist from doing D

(b) to deter U from doing D in the future.

It is too strong to hold that the *de facto* ruler must *know* that the undergoer of hardship is "guilty" for infliction of hardship to constitute punishment. That X punishes Y only if X knows that Y is "guilty" implies that X punishes Y only if Y is truly guilty. Usage does *not* support this implication. "I was punished for something I didn't do," is a report of an injustice done, not a misuse of words. Moreover, it would be a mistake to hold that punishment is unjustified unless the punisher knows that the accused is "guilty." Occasionally, one is justified in punishing even though one does not have adequate evidence of "guilt." For example, while under attack by the enemy, a sergeant boots a soldier in the tail to get him to desist from what looks like cowering; actually, the soldier wasn't cowering but uttering the briefest of prayers. But, the sergeant was justified in his punishment; he simply didn't have time to check the facts. Of course, the extent of punishment justifiable in cases of inadequate evidence is clearly tempered by that lack.

I conclude that Professor Ducasse's definition *excludes* cases properly called cases of punishment. The most which is inductively warranted is that the *de facto* ruler *believes* the undergoer of hardship "guilty"; otherwise we have not punishment but the gratuitous infliction of hardship. Next, consider the third clause of the definition. It is not enough to refer to the deterrence from the particular kind of wrongdoing already done. As Professor Ducasse later indicates, it is the *tendency* toward wrongdoing which one often purposes to change. So, at least where the punished beings are capable of being deterred from a kind of activity not necessarily identical with a specific deed (D) it would be in the spirit of what Professor Ducasse goes on to say to broaden the scope of what it is the punishments purpose to deter; so, 3(b) might read: ". . . to deter U from doing D and other associated wrongdoings in the future."

Next, an example follows which establishes that Professor Ducasse's definition includes as punishment what usage refuses to account as punishment. Imagine a woman, Mary, who unknowingly has been infecting many others with typhoid. Discovered, she is forcibly detained in quarantine, deprived of freedom of movement and conversation, something she dislikes intensely. Everyone strongly disapproves of what Mary has been doing, namely, going about in public contaminating people; thus, in Professor Ducasse's terms, Mary is "guilty" of causing an epidemic. Moreover, the immediate purpose of inflicting the hardship of quarantine on her is to prevent her from infecting others, i.e., to cause her to desist what she was doing and to deter her from doing that in the future.

Now, although this example fits Professor Ducasse's definition of *punishment,* it is obvious, I submit, that it would be a mistake to say. "Mary was punished for causing a typhoid epidemic." Why? Because Mary was not *responsible* for what she did; nobody could possibly think Mary deserved punishment. She did not know she was infecting others, did not know she had typhoid, and was not in a position wherein she could be held responsible, even though ignorant of what she was doing.[1] Mary was not punished but quarantined.

To be brief I maintain that someone, *X,* by bringing about the purposeful infliction of hardship on another, *Y,* has punished *Y* only if *X* believes that *Y* deserves that hardship. Otherwise, what is lost is the distinction between *punishment* and *treatment.*

One way to locate the difference between Professor Ducasse and me is to note that for him "guilt" consists solely in having done something of which a *de facto* ruler disapproves. But usage does not support this. For example, imagine *X* is headmaster of a preparatory school. One of his duties is to punish infractions of the rules legislated by the board of governors. He does not disapprove of smoking in the lavatories; indeed, he thinks the rule against it is a bad one and is doing what he can do to have it revoked. But one of his charges, *Y,* is caught smoking in a lavatory and *X* discharges his duty by imposing the prescribed punishment of restricting *Y* from going to town on Saturdays. Has *X* punished *Y?* Indeed. Why? Because *X* had discharged his duty in the prescribed way: *X* imposed hardship on *Y* because *X* knew that *Y* had done something which, according to the rules *X* was committed to enforce, was a punishable offence.

The concept of punishment is, among humans, intimately involved with systems of rules, duly constituted legislative bodies, duly appointed judges and executors. This is simply absent from Professor Ducasse's considerations. What happens is that the notion of *desert* is deserted.

Unless I misread him, the reason Professor Ducasse leaves off any consideration of desert is because he believes it to be inextricably bound to the theory of punishment known as *"retributivist."* And, since he identifies that theory as ". . . the same as that set forth in . . . Leviticus . . ." (the *lex talionis*—an odious and impossible view) he dispenses with desert entirely. But, it is a mistake to suppose that the retributivist must hold to the law of the talon; the only thing necessary is to hold that there be a *proportion* between the severity of punishment and the severity of wrongdoing.² Without the retributivist's notion of desert, I say, not punishment, but, at best, treatment.

Let me sum up by replying to Professor Ducasse's challenge to the retributivist. He asks what the retributivist would do if there were available a pill which, taken, would change ". . . the most vicious of criminals into a saint. Ought the criminal then be made to swallow the pill, instead of being punished? Or ought he to be punished anyway, since he 'deserves' it, and not given the pill?" My reply is the criminal deserves to be punished; that the most effective way to do it would be to make him take the pill, thereby effectively depriving the criminal of something essentially his —his personality. To regard this as anything other than punishment is to alter seriously an attitude I think most worthy of keeping: that attitude out of which we can regard others as persons, not things to be manipulated according to our whims, providing we have enough power to be *de facto* rulers. In short, *de facto* is not enough with punishment; *de juris* absolutely must be involved if there is to be punishment at all. Thus, the concept of *desert* must be accounted its place in any definition of *punishment*.

References

1. HART, H. L. A.: Negligence, *mens rea,* and criminal responsibility. Reprinted in S. Morgenbesser and J. Walsh (Eds.): *Free Will,* Englewood Cliffs, Prentice-Hall, 1962. This last proviso is included to honor the point made by Hart that one may be held responsible for something even though ignorant that that something was occurring; e.g., a switchman who falls asleep on the job is nonetheless

responsible for a train wreck which results from his failing to do his job because it is his job not to fall asleep but to perform his duties as switchman.

2. ARMSTRONG, K. G.: The retributivist hits back. *Mind, 70*:486, 1961.

COMMENTARY ON DUCASSE'S "PHILOSOPHY AND WISDOM IN PUNISHMENT AND REWARD"

LLEWELLYN GROSS

An invitation to comment on Professor Ducasse's paper provides both the occasion and the opportunity to express appreciation for the excellence of his scholarship. Not only am I sympathetic with the assumptions, style of reasoning, and conclusions of his paper, but I welcome the quality of good sentiment which pervades it.

After reading Professor Ducasse's careful analysis I wondered if I might have failed to understand, through no fault of his, the basis upon which his definition of punishment rests. I take it he means to derive his definition by induction from a representative sample of scientific and common sense usages. But I do not know whether he includes as a necessary step in this process the "reconstruction" of both usages. I shall assume, however, that he accepts the reconstructionist version of analysis, for only by doing so could he have succeeded so well in offering insights not found in dictionary definitions.

Most dictionaries take punishment to be a consequence of violation of law, of refusal to obey rules or regulations, of disobedience to authority, or of intentional wrong doing. According to *The American College Dictionary,* "To punish is chiefly to inflict penalty or pain as a retribution for misdeeds, with little or no expectation of correction or improvement." When the aim of controlling or reforming the offender is salient, the terms *discipline* or *correction* appear to be common usages. It may be noted that these definitions are, on the whole, compatible with the main theses of the article in the *Journal of Philosophy* mentioned by Professor Ducasse. He points out that the British philosophers cited in the article assume that punishment is always of some human being by some human agent; also, that punishment is inherently always for violation of some moral or legal rule. Professor Ducasse believes that these two assumptions greatly limit the applicability of the term, since human beings may punish animals and animals may punish either other animals or human beings. In general, he holds that the applicability of the term punishment is "substantially wider" than British philosophers recognize. Since this question is central to Ducasse's discussion, my comments are directed principally to it.

Perhaps the most interesting aspect of Professor Ducasse's definition of punishment is its emphasis upon the purposive infliction of pain, loss, suffering, deprivation or other hardship on the undergoer. Punishment is inflicted to cause the wrongdoer to desist and to deter him from repeating the disapproved thing. In a later paragraph, Professor Ducasse reinforces this point by stating that punishment is necessarily heterotelic; it occurs only if it is performed ". . . for the sake of some effect which the activity causes." Thus, suffering is not punishment when it is unintended or when it is performed for its own sake. This requirement is illuminating. It tells us that the academic man who "perishes" for want of publications is punished. It tells us that the victims of auto accidents, whether drivers or passengers, are not punished except for contributory negligence. What, on the other hand, can be said about the mass killing of minority groups which has occurred, periodically, throughout human history? Whether justified or unjustified, was the extinction of these groups done for its own sake or for some effect? To some observers, the release of repressed hostilities appears to be as strong a motive for the destruction of minorities as the elimination of competition or the establishment of "racial purity."

Professor Ducasse states that infliction of a hardship for its own sake *(qua autotelic)* is not punitive but sadistic or masochistic. Should we conclude, then, that the destruction of minorities for the purpose of eliminating competition is an instance of punishment rather than sadism? Subsequently, Professor Ducasse states that a dictator, simply by virtue of having autocratic power, can punish a slave or animal for having done something the ruler happened to dislike. The act may be independent of any rule of conduct or morality promulgated by the ruler. In these terms, was the destruction of the American Indian in the nineteenth century, and the European Jew in the twentieth century, a case of sadism or punishment? Insofar as their destruction resulted from dislike on the part of rulers or their agents, it may have been punishment, but very often it was punishment for merely existing as a sentient being rather than for acting in disapproved ways. However, "punishment" for merely existing seems to warrant the appellation of purposelessness, and hence the interpretation of sadism. It is worthy of note that many humanists have called the annihilation of racial minorities acts of sadism rather than punishment. Punishment seems to suggest the righteous response of legitimate authority toward a transgressor, one who is believed to have done something "bad." If it is not bestowed upon a "bad" man it is, at least, bestowed upon one who has broken a law—a "criminal."[1]

The preceding line of thought returns us to the legal view of punishment discussed earlier. In this connection, let us compare Professor Ducasse's use of punishment with that offered by criminologists Sutherland and Cressey.[2] The latter hold that two essential ideas are contained in the concept of punishment as an instrument of criminal law and public justice:

1. It is inflicted by the group in its corporate capacity upon one who is regarded as a member of the same group.
2. It involves pain or suffering produced by design and justified by some value that the suffering is assumed to have.

On this definition, ". . . war is not punishment for in war the action is directed against foreigners." The authors state, additionally, that ". . . three types of wrongs, followed by three types of reactions, no one of which is clearly punitive, may be found in preliterate societies."

The first includes tribal and social offenses, such as treason, witchcraft, sacrilege, and poisoning. The reaction of annihilation followed from regarding the offender as an enemy, or as one who polluted society, or as one who must be sacrificed to please the gods.

The second group of wrongs were injuries to private individuals who were not in the same family. The reaction to these feuds was not a societal one, since the general community was merely a spectator.

The third group of wrongs consisted of injuries to other

members of the same family. Ridicule was the most powerful method of control and was generally sufficient to secure
observance of rules. In these nonliterate groups, the authors
claim, certain motives and attitudes can be found ". . . which
apparently preceded the punitive reaction to lawbreaking but
were not, in themselves, punishment. . . . It was not until
the modern period that the clearly punitive reaction to crime
—the purposive infliction of pain on the offender because
of some assumed value of the pain—became popular."[3]

I mention Sutherland and Cressey because their views differ
from Professor Ducasse's in essential ways. All three types of
reaction to the wrongs mentioned by Sutherland and Cressey are
cases of punishment in Professor Ducasse's formulation. That
they do not constitute punishment for Sutherland and Cressey
does not mean that Professor Ducasse is mistaken. Both
analyses are valuable from a pedagogic and scientific standpoint.
My own preference is nearer to Professor Ducasse's views, if I
understand him correctly. If we do not regard the preceding reactions as cases of punishment we must, perhaps, deny that any
body but a societal or corporal group has ever inflicted punishment.
It seems to me such an interpretation, with its suggestion of
social sanction, would come dangerously close to justifying all
forms of punishment. In the language of politics, or rather one
version of it, the State can do no wrong. However, in ordinary
usage, punishment seems to connote some degree of legitimacy,
of "just deserts," and for this reason I would qualify Professor
Ducasse's thesis that any form of purposeful harm should be
called *punishment.*

I turn now to one of the characteristics mentioned by Professor
Ducasse as essential for an entity to be capable of punishment, *viz:*
it must be such that infliction upon it of experiences it dislikes
causes it to stop its wrongdoing, and conditions it against repeating
the wrongdoing in the future. Professor Ducasse applies this requirement to prisoners and concludes that since imprisonment fails
to correct the majority—they are often repeaters—their hardship is
not really punishment. It may be noted without implying disapproval that this interpretation is at variance with both everyday

and criminological usage. In both usages, imprisonment is always punishment, except in the special case where prison life provides release from the insecurity or suffering which characterized the individual's existence outside of prison. The situation of patients in mental hospitals is more ambiguous. Although many remain uncured, confinement is not usually regarded as punishment. However, in a somewhat earlier period of our history and now quite recently, sociologists are viewing hospital confinement as somewhat like punishment. Goffman's description of a mental hospital may be taken as illustrative:

> The patient's life is regulated and ordered according to a disciplinarian system developed for the management by a small staff of a large number of involuntary inmates. In this system the attendant is likely to be the key staff person, informing the patient of the punishments and rewards that are to regulate his life and arranging for medical authorization for such privileges and punishment. Quiet, obedient behavior leads to the patient's promotion in the ward system; obstreperous, untidy behavior to demotion.[4]

Given, finally, the interesting similarities and differences between Professor Ducasse's definition of punishment and those to which I have referred, how are we to judge the suitability of such common phrases as "threat of punishment," "publicity without punishment," "punishment in itself," "the impulse to punish," "God's punishment," or simply "the idea of eternal punishment"? And consider the more literary expressions: punished by misfortune; death is no punishment; let the punishment fit the crime; sent heavenward for punishment. Neither Epictetus' words "forgiveness is better than punishment" nor the psychoanalytic preference for "self-inflicted" or "internal" punishment appear to fit well into Professor Ducasse's formulation. Nevertheless, many distinguished thinkers seem to be largely on the side of Professor Ducasse. Plato, among others, held: "It is as expedient that a wicked man be punished as that a sick man be cured by a physician: for all chastisement is a kind of medicine." Seneca expressed this utilitarian idea even more clearly when he wrote, "We will not punish a man because he hath offended, but that he may offend no more," And if a further illustration is desired, consider Voltaire, who remarked, "The punishment of criminals should be of use; when a man is hanged he is good for nothing."

References

1. MABBOTT, J. D.: Punishment. In F. A. Olafson (Ed.): *Justice and Social Policy*. Englewood Cliffs, Prentice-Hall, 1961, p. 41.
2. SUTHERLAND, E. H. and CRESSEY, D. G.: *Principles of Criminology,* 5th ed. New York, Lippincott, 1955, pp. 256-59.
3. *Ibid.,* p. 259.
4. GOFFMAN, E.: Asylums. Reprinted in B. Rosenberg, I. Gerver and F. W. Howton (Eds.): *Mass Society in Crisis*. New York, Macmillan, 1964, p. 189.

REPLY TO COMMENTS

C. J. DUCASSE

I turn first to Professor Pratt's statement on his first page that, as he interprets the point of the last sections of my address, I am obliged to answer the following question: "What, in modern-day circumstances in our society, would, on the whole, be the wisest way to punish those who break the laws of our society, given the means available to us?" This, however, is not a correct statement of that with which I am actually concerned. It is, instead: What, given the means available to us, would, on the whole, be the wisest way, or ways, *to treat* persons of diverse kinds who break the laws of our society? The wisest way might, in a given case, be medication, psychiatric treatment, or perhaps punishment. But, if it is punishment, then it must be punishment intelligent enough in timing, in kind, in magnitude, and in frequency to be effective; i.e., to be reformatory to some extent and, to that extent, to protect society—which, as Hal Hollister says rightly, ". . . is the one overall goal that makes sense of a prison system."

To Professor Pratt's next comment, my reply would be that my definition of the term punishment is (or seeks to be) non-arbitrary in that it attempts to apply not only to cases of punishment of a human being by other human beings, but to *all* cases of punishment. These, as I pointed out, include cases of punishment of animals by humans, of humans by animals, and of animals by other animals; whereas Professor Pratt's comment takes into consideration, arbitrarily, only cases of punishment of humans by other humans.

A word next concerning his statement that "usage" (I would say, undiscriminative usage) does not support my contention that punishment presupposes guilt. He writes that the statement, "I was punished for something I did not do," is not a misuse of words. I reply that the correct wording to use in that statement instead of "I was punished" would have been "I was maltreated," or "I was made to undergo hardship" for having done something I did not do. And this, let it be noted, is still a statement of an injustice done: it *is* unjust to impose hardship on a person for having done something which in fact he did not do— and it is unjust even though it is not properly termed *punishment.* Ordinary usage is undiscriminating in that it fails to differentiate between punishing as against imposing hardship for some purpose other than punishing.

As regards Professor Pratt's contention that for imposition of hardship to be warranted when punishment is intended it is not necessary for the *de facto* ruler to *know* the undergoer is guilty, but only for the ruler to *believe* him guilty, my answer is this: if *R merely believes but does not really know* what the undergoer *(U)* of the hardship imposed on him by *R did do,* i.e., was really guilty of the wrong for which *R* intends to punish him, then imposition of that hardship is not really punishment but is *merely believed* by *R* to be punishment. Imposing hardship on a being who is not guilty of doing what the hardship is imposed for is not actually punishing him, but is only maltreating him unjustly.

I turn next to the case of the woman, Mary, who unknowingly and unintentionally has been infecting many others with typhoid, and who, when this is discovered, is quarantined, which is a species of hardship. Professor Pratt's commentary states that this case fits my definition of punishment, but this is an error. The quarantine does not (as the commentary asserts it does) cause Mary to *desist* from spreading typhoid nor does it *deter* her from doing so in the future. These two terms presuppose that the behavior desisted and/or deterred from is specifically an *act;* i.e., it is voluntarily engaged in by the person concerned for the purpose of causing by means of it an effect that person desires. *This was not so in Mary's case.** The quarantine does not, *psychologically,* make Mary *desist,* nor *deter* her from spreading typhoid, but simply *prevents* her, *physically,* from doing so. And there are many cases where imposition of a hardship is not punishment nor intended to be so, but is imposed simply because of certain effects it will have, effects desirable, but not otherwise obtainable. An instance, which I cite in my reply to Professor Gross's comments, is the drafting of men into the armed forces. It is a hardship on the men drafted, but is neither sadistic nor punitive, and is imposed as the only means available of providing in sufficient size the armed forces the nation needs. One must distinguish here between purposing to inflict hardship, and inflicting hardship for a purpose.

I pass now to the case offered by Professor Pratt as refuting my contention that doing something of which the *de facto* ruler disapproves constitutes guilt; namely, the case of a school whose board of governors ruled that students shall not smoke in the lavatories; and whose headmaster, although he thinks that rule is a bad one, nevertheless punishes a student who violated the rule.

This case, however, does not refute my contention because the *de facto* ruler in that school is its board of governors, not its headmaster, who is only its employee, one of whose assigned tasks is to enforce *their* rules.

Again, I do not, as Professor Pratt's commentary charges, ignore the fact that in human society there are rules passed by legislative bodies for punishment of conduct of certain kinds. My definition of punishment fits that fact, but in addition it also fits many others which greatly differ from it, yet are patently cases of punishment. Nor do I eliminate the notion of *desert,* but employ it, tacitly, when I say that a person cannot be punished, but only maltreated unjustly, unless he is guilty (i.e., has actually done something disapproved by the ruler) *and* his personality is such that infliction of hardship on him—if, as I specify, it is intelligent

---

*See my article "Substants, Capacities, and Tendencies" *Review of Metaphysics,* September, 1964, pp. 28, 29.

in timing, in kind, in magnitude, and in frequency—causes him psychologically to desist from his present wrongdoing and conditions him to some extent against repetition of that wrongdoing. If these several conditions are satisfied in a given case, then the person concerned *deserves* punishment. Retributionists have no monopoly on the notion of "desert," but only on a merely emotional conception of "desert."

Finally, a word concerning Professor Pratt's statement of what should be done to an inveterate criminal, and why, in the highly hypothetical case of the availability of a pill, the taking of which would immediately and permanently turn the worst criminal into a saint.

Professor Pratt would make the criminal take the pill. The reason he gives is that the criminal ought to be punished, and that his being turned into a saint by the pill would be punishment because it would deprive him of his particular personality (which happens to be a vicious one).

To this I reply that, having become a saint, he would not miss that vicious personality; and that elimination of it, since it would not be experience of a hardship, would not constitute punishment. Anyway, Professor Pratt's aversion, which I share, to the idea of manipulation of persons "according to our whims" does not apply to manipulation of persons *not* according to our whims, but according to what the good of society may make necessary. Sentencing a criminal to imprisonment *is* an attempt to manipulate him psychologically for the good of society. In the majority of cases it is not very effectively reformative. But if it is nevertheless justified, why not instead use the pill if it should become available, since *ex hypothesi* it would be completely effective?

The basis on which my definition of *punishment* rests is a conspectus of all the kinds of cases commonly acknowledged to be cases of punishment. These include not only the cases where punishment is of some human being by a human being or human agency for violation of some moral or legal rule, but also cases where punishment is of an animal by a human being, or of a human being by an animal, or of an animal by another animal. The dictionary definitions cited by Professor Gross fit only *some* of these kinds of cases. But H. C. Warren's *Dictionary of Psychology* (p. 219) gives a much more inclusive definition of punishment:

"1. the infliction of pain or discomfort upon an organism in consequence of the violation of a regulation, or following a course of action not desired by the inflictor; 2. a negative motivating stimulus, e.g., electric shock. [Applied both to social and legal procedure and to educational methods with human children and criminals, and in animal learning. The term harks back to the traditional notion of retribution, but has been retained in psychology to denote a method of deterrence and of learning.]" The definition of "reward" (p. 234) is correspondingly inclusive.*

I turn now to the meaning of my specification that punishment is heterotelic. I am afraid that what I wrote about this in the paragraph to which Professor Gross refers (the first paragraph of my address under "The Purposiveness of Punishment") was not explicit enough to make clear that what he later describes as "Ducasse's thesis that any form of purposeful harm should be called 'punishment' " is, on the contrary, no thesis of mine and is something I would emphatically deny.

It was in order to forestall such a possible misinterpretation (after saying at the end of the paragraph to which Professor Gross refers, that purposive causation of an experience disliked by the undergoer of it can be punishment *only if* it is heterotelic) that I added the parenthesis: "(. . . but is not necessarily punishment *if* . . .)" it is heterotelic. In short, all punishment is heterotelic causation of hardship, but *not all heterotelic causation of hardship is punishment*.

Examples making the latter evident are numerous. One would be that the charging of high prices for drugs or hospital accommodation *is* causation of hardship to sick persons who are not wealthy; but this is not punishment, since its purpose is not to make them desist from taking the drugs they need nor to deter them from going to a hospital when they need an operation. The purpose of charging those high prices is to pay for the high cost of discovering, creating, and distributing those drugs, and of

---

*F. A. Logan and A. R. Wagner, *Reward and Punishment*, Boston, Allyn and Bacon, 1965. The psychology of reward and punishment is here extensively discussed.

providing the facilities and personnel which are possible only in a hospital. The Medicare provisions are not intended to *exculpate* the poor of their costly sickness but simply to *alleviate* the hardship which that costliness constitutes.

Another patent example of causation of hardship which is heterotelic but does not constitute punishing is the drafting of men into the nation's armed forces. This hardship is caused them neither sadistically nor punitively but because the nation needs armed forces and the draft is the only means of providing them in sufficient size.

Once it is realized there are many cases of heterotelic causing of hardship which (for the same reason as in the two just mentioned) are not cases of punishment, it becomes evident that my contention that all punishment is heterotelic is not impugned at all by any of the cases Professor Gross adduces, none of which would commonly be regarded as cases of punishment. They would have to be so regarded *only if* all causation of hardship with a purpose were *eo ipso* punishment; and this I not only do *not* contend but have already cited cases showing it to be false.

Since I agree the cases mentioned by Professor Gross are not cases of punishment, there is no need for me to discuss all of them. I shall therefore limit myself to considering briefly the case of the professor who did not publish much if at all and was not promoted; and to saying a few words as to the conditions under which it would, or would not, be a case of punishment.

That a professor P who had published little or nothing was not promoted is not necessarily punishment any more than if the reason for his not being promoted had been that the college did not have the money for the higher salary of the higher rank. Or there may have been money enough for only one promotion, so that some other member of the staff was the one promoted instead of professor P, perhaps because he had published more, or because he was a better teacher, or had seniority, or because he was better qualified in some other respect.

Nonpromotion of professor P because he had not published much would have been a case of punishment if the purpose of withholding promotion had been to deter him from persisting in his failure to publish, and this had somehow become known to him.

II

IMMORALITY, CRIME, AND TREATMENT

Charles A. Baylis

Code De Trypheme
I. Ne nuis pas à ton voisin,
II. Ceci bien compris, fais ce qu'il te plait.
Pierre Louys, *Les Aventures du Roi Pausole*

It would be relatively easy to define *punishment* in such a way that every case of it would be justifiable, and equally easy to define it in a manner that would allow for no instance of it to be justifiable. But either of these approaches would beg, by verbal fiat, the very questions we are most interested in raising and discussing. We seek, rather, an approach which will help us distinguish between justifiable and unjustifiable goals and methods of punishment. For such reasons I hazard the following broad account.

The Nature of Punishment

Though we can, and sometimes do, speak of punishment of or by a group or a class or organization of people, or by a corporation or a state or some other abstract entity, punishment nevertheless is always initiated by individuals, and sooner or later falls on individuals. I propose, therefore, to limit my account to the paradigm case of the punishment of one sentient individual by another. I use the expression "sentient individual" to refer not only to members of *homo sapiens* but also to members of other species capable of sense or feeling. This usage conforms to our ordinary way of speaking about an animal trainer punishing his charges, or of one of us finding it necessary or desirable in the course of training, to punish a household pet.

To punish a sentient creature involves at a minimum: (a) inflicting some harm or restraint (not necessarily physical) upon it, and (b) doing so, in part at least, because of some harm which that individual is believed to have caused. Furthermore, we do not ordinarily call such an act "punishment" unless we believe it to be motivated, at least to some degree, by a desire to improve the behavior of the individual punished. Even when we execute a criminal we offer the excuse that we have improved his behavior by rendering it nonexistent. By contrast, a purely reflexive slap, though it is caused, is not motivated; it has no purpose, though it may serve a useful function. In what follows, I shall be concerned primarily with legal punishment authorized by law, though I shall sometimes make use of an instance of nonlegal punishment to highlight the legal case. The number of philosophical topics which bear on punishment is large, but I limit my discussion to:

1. *Moral responsibility, free will, and determinism*
2. *The contrast between crime and immorality*
3. *An evaluation of current types of criminal punishment together with recommendations for the future.*

Moral Responsibility, Freedom, and Determinism

Careful discussions of punishment and its justifiability raise various problems about the responsibility of the wrongdoer. A minimum requirement for legal responsibility is that the offending act be a voluntary one, not the result of merely involuntary muscular movements as in sleep-walking, or automatism, or reflex action. Another common requirement for criminal responsibility is the presence of certain "mental elements" in the wrongdoer. Lawyers and philosophers of law use the phrase *mens rea* (a guilty mind) as a general name to designate such mental elements. The point of this requirement is to rule out guilt for accidental events, and psychotic agents. It is not enough actually to kill someone in order to be tried for murder; it must be shown that the agent did not act unintentionally, or while mentally incapacitated.[1]

Admittedly, to know the motives and/or causes of what is going on in another's mind is at best difficult, and often, in practice, impossible. Hence, a more recent view, and one growing in popularity, has been strongly argued in Britain in recent years by, among others, Lady Wootton.[2] According to this view, proof of *mens rea* is not necessary to make the use of legal sanctions relevant. As long as a person's act is shown in court to fit the legal definition of a crime, he *qualifies* for such sanctions. These may be either punitive or therapeutic in nature, or both; or, depending upon the special nature of the case, neither, in which case the offender is discharged.[3] The point is that the judgment of what to do should be made in terms of forward-looking considerations about what would likely have the best consequences both for the offender and for society. H. L. A. Hart, however, is unwilling to go quite this far.[4] He writes that if we imprison an offender in order to deter him and, by example, deter others, then we are using him for the benefit of society and this behavior would not be justifiable unless we could show that the person so treated was a responsible agent.

He argues also that many crimes involve in their definition reference to intention or some other mental element, *e.g.*, the idea of an attempt to commit a crime.[5] As a third difficulty he notes that in many instances only *intention* serves to distinguish an accidental blow from an assault.[6]

Hart's conclusion, therefore, is essentially this: Emphasis on the consequences of proposed punishment is of primary importance, both for a criminal and for society. But we cannot give up entirely our efforts to discern some things about the mind of the accused. For there are some sorts of crime that cannot be defined without reference to the intent of the accused. And further, we cannot justly punish a man for the sake of deterring others unless we have at least some good evidence that he need not have acted as he did, that he could have acted otherwise. In at least these two respects, Hart holds, knowledge of the state of mind of the accused is needed for a justified decision as to his guilt, and for the selection of justified punishment. *But once the prisoner is properly found guilty, whether he should be treated therapeutically or penally or both, and in what ways, is a matter of maximizing the good these treatments will provide for him and for others who will be affected.*

Very different from these problems are those which arise about responsibility when they are considered by philosophers who are concerned about the implications of a deterministic theory of volition as contrasted with a free will account. Extreme "free-willists" contend that a person cannot properly be held responsible for his choices unless they are completely undetermined and thus are, in that sense, "really free," for any effective degree of influence limits a person's freedom to at least that extent. On this view, not even his own character or interests can determine a person's choices without infringing on his freedom. Actually in this type of view, a person can choose freely only if *nothing* determines his choice. More moderate free-willists sometimes admit a person's choice can still be free even though there are influences which *incline* him toward one alternative rather than another, as long as they do not determine his choice. But any consideration inclining him toward one alternative strongly enough to determine his choice *ipso facto* deprives him of that choice of freedom. It seems to follow from this that influences which are ineffective do not deprive one of freedom, but influences which are effective, do. Thus, if one is faced with a difficult but important choice, and prudently investigates the alternatives thoroughly and then, on the evidence thus uncovered, reaches a wise decision, he has not decided as a truly free man would. But surely such a conclusion is the *reductio ad absurdum* of the view that a person's will is free only if nothing causally affects his choice.

My own suggestion for escaping the difficulties involved is to accept a thoroughgoing deterministic theory which will hold for every event in the universe, whether a human being is involved or not. How to state such a theory accurately and precisely is beyond my powers. I also gather from dipping into the works of professional philosophers of science that there is a good deal of disagreement among them as to just how such a very general principle should be stated. But the sort of thing we are looking for seems clear enough and can be indicated even by an amateur in technical scientific matters. Determinists believe in something like the uniformity of nature. They regard all natural changes as lawful, and man as a part of nature. His choices and his actions, like all other natural events, occur in accordance with natural laws. We know many of the laws which govern human behavior, including physical and physiological ones, for example. We know a good deal less about the laws of human motivation, about unconscious desires, about valid psychiatric generalizations, and so on. But in all these areas we are learning more and more. Even in cases of human behavior where, at present, our most knowledgeable scientists do not yet know enough to make reliable predictions, they tend to regard such knowledge as theoretically obtainable even if it is now beyond our reach.

It is a matter of common knowledge, I take it, that even Heisenberg's famous "Principle of Indeterminacy" does not entail the absence of lawful behavior on the part of subatomic particles. If I understand his principle correctly, it is to this effect: the more accurately we can pinpoint the position of, say, an electron, the less accurately we can specify its speed and direction of motion, and vice versa. This limitation indicates, however, not a lack of lawful behavior, but a regularly present kind of observational difficulty. To realize the conditions of observation of one variable makes impossible the accurate determination of the other, and vice versa. But there seems to be no need to suppose that the actual, though unknown, value of either of these variables is indeterminate. It is simply in certain circumstances indeterminable in the sense of being unspecifiable. Indeed, the very fact that we can determine either variable suggests both are determinate.

Quite a different type of fear, expressed by some indeterminists, is that if determinism were true, our choices would be so controlled that at least, in certain cases, we could not choose what we most want to choose. But this, I believe, is clearly a mistake. Consider the kinds of freedom we have in connection with choice and action:

We have complete freedom of choice in the sense that in any situation which presents several alternatives, any one of which we can choose of we wish, we can and always do choose the one we prefer to choose. If Mary says, "I don't want to marry John, but I have to," we understand her to mean that if the situation were other than it is she would choose not to marry him. But being what it is, she chooses to marry him.

Can we do what we choose? Yes, but within limits. I can choose meaningfully to return to Durham tomorrow by plane or I can choose to go by train, but because I cannot run a mile in four minutes it would be silly of me to say I choose to do so. We have freedom of action only within limits. Do we have freedom of rational motivation, or, if you prefer, freedom from irrational motivation? Here again the answer is, Yes, within limits. These tend to be set by a person's early background and training, but with good will and practice he can improve his behavior in this respect. He can learn not to make difficult and important choices until he has investigated the available alternatives and weighed as best he can the values of each. Because he learns from his mistakes, his ability to choose wisely gradually improves; then he is influenced by this improved self to take further steps toward becoming the self to which he has learned to aspire.

In short, therefore, determinism leaves us all the freedoms we value most: the freedoms of choice, action, and rational motivation. We can learn to think reasonably and we can learn to act rationally. By contrast, if some of our decisions occurred uncaused and unmotivated, we could never be sure what we might say or do next. A will that "pops off" without cause or reason would indeed render us irresponsible whenever it took over. We should all hope that determinism is true.

Crime and Immorality

There is a growing interest in British legal and humanitarian circles in distinguishing crime, *i.e.,* the breaking of laws, from immorality, *i.e.,* the breaking of generally accepted and widely supported moral precepts. In a recent volume, Professor H. L. A. Hart has indicated incisively his own approval of this distinction and his strong opposition to the legal enforcement of morality.[7] He refers appreciatively to the Suicide Act of 1961 which removes the penalties of criminal law from an act clearly condemned by conventional morality. He points out that many people hope such reform measures may be extended to certain forms of abortion, homosexual behavior between consenting adults in private, and to certain forms of euthanasia. The misery caused by punishing these acts outweighs any conceivable harm they may do.

The principal argument against making such conduct (widely regarded as immoral) a legally punishable crime was stated explicitly about a hundred years ago by John Stuart Mill:

The only purpose for which power can rightfully be exercised over any member of a civilized community against his will is to prevent harm to others. . . . His own good either physical or moral is not a

sufficient warrant. He cannot rightfully be compelled to do or for-
bear because it will be better for him to do so, because it will make
him happier, because in the opinions of others, to do so would be
wise or even right.[8]

That there is genuine need to recall Mill's strong position is
indicated, H. L. A. Hart notes, by the 1961-1962 case in the House
of Lords of *Shaw v. Director of Public Prosecutions*. In this case,
the House of Lords resurrected from the eighteenth century the
notion that "conspiracy to corrupt public morals" constitutes a
common-law offense.[9] California and other states of the Union,
Hart notes, also include in their calendar of crime a conspiracy to
injure public morals. In most cases these laws are dead letters, but
not in England. There, all that needs be established is that the
accused agreed to do or say something which a jury thought might
lead someone else morally astray.[10] Hart concludes that Mill would
have been dismayed by such procedures because they authorize
gross invasions of individual liberty, while Bentham would have
been equally dismayed because they disregard the legal values of
certainty and extend what he called *"ex post facto* law."[11]

Fortunately, there are also more liberal pressures at work in
England. In 1954, a committee which became well-known as the
Wolfenden Committee, was appointed to consider the law and
practice relative to (a) homosexual offenses, and (b) prostitution
and solicitation therefore.[12]

As to prostitution, they recommend unanimously that though
prostitution should not be made illegal, public soliciting should
be forbidden as an offensive nuisance to ordinary citizens. This
recommendation has since become law. As to homosexuality, they
recommended, 12 to 1, that homosexual practices between consenting adults in private should no longer be a crime. Bills to
this end have passed the House of Lords several times but none
has yet passed the House of Commons. Such a bill, however, was
introduced into the Commons on July 5, 1966, by a vote of 244
to 100. Whether "time will be found" for it to reach final passage
before adjournment is, at the date of writing, still problematical.
But support for it has increased considerably.

The Wolfenden Committee gives as its own most "decisive"

reason for its recommendation the importance which society and the law ought to give to individual freedom of choice and action in matters of private morality:

> Unless a deliberate attempt is to be made by society, acting through the agency of the law, to equate the sphere of crime with that of sin, there must remain a realm of private morality and immorality which is, in brief and crude terms, not the law's business. To say this is not to condone or encourage private immorality. On the contrary, to emphasize the personal and private nature of moral or immoral conduct is to emphasise the personal and private responsibility of the individual for his own actions, and that is a responsibility which a mature agent can properly be expected to carry for himself without the threat of punishment from the law.[13]

Hart reports that these developments in England have had close parallels in America. In 1955, the American Law Institute recommended that all consensual relations between adults in private should be exempt from the range of criminal law on the ground that no harm to the community is involved in such practices, while interference with them produces real harm. The recommendation was hotly debated and finally accepted by a majority vote of 35 to 24.[14]

Among the principal arguments for making legal crimes of particular types of action which are widely and strongly disapproved by a majority of society, the following are outstanding:

1. Since such acts are regarded as immoral and wicked by a majority of the society, it seems reasonable to add legal sanctions to this general moral disapproval, and thus encourage conformity to the approved modes of behavior. This additional pressure may deter people who might not be moved to obedience merely by social disapproval. Making a crime of the sinful act may thus decrease the number of sinners.

2. Lord Devlin and others take it for granted that any society has the right to seek to preserve its existence. Since, according to him, immorality, like treason, can jeopardize a society's existence, it is important and justifiable to make action thus inimical to the society a crime as well as a sin.

However, there are much stronger reasons for retaining the distinction between sins and crimes:

The use of legal coercion by a society calls for justification as being *prima facie* objectionable and thus to be tolerated only for the sake of some compensatory good. The punishment of offenders involves harming them and is, to that extent, bad.

The coercion of other members of society by the threat of punishment limits their freedom of choice; this restriction also needs to be balanced by some countervailing good.

Many moral principles are very vague and if laws are made of them the punitive authorities must be given overly wide discretionary powers in deciding which acts fall under these laws. This defect also involves breaches of the legal principle that what is forbidden should be incisively defined.

Moral precepts concerning sexual behavior impose especially difficult burdens. Except in very homogeneous societies sexual morals differ widely among different sub-groups of the society. For example, Catholic rules tend to be much more restrictive than Unitarian ones, oriental rules very different from western ones.[15]

In short, there is much to be said for keeping the list of crimes clear and brief and leaving room for a good deal of variety of opinion about detailed moral matters. Retaining the finely balanced distinction between immorality and crime may well serve to reduce the psychiatric difficulties under which many people suffer severely. Thus, no harm to the secular interests of the community is involved in most atypical sex practices in private between consenting adult partners. Moreover, realization of this can considerably diminish guilt feelings and the harm they do.

The kind of moral problems which in practice prove most perplexing for conscientious persons are seldom those of a broad generic sort. Instead they tend to be quite specific: What, in this situation, is the morally right thing to do? Most of the time we should be only too glad to do what is right if we could just know what the right course of action is. Here, perhaps, more help is needed from philosophers who deal with ethical and moral questions. It would be useful if they illustrated more often their abstract ethical rules by developing the implications of their doctrines so that they would be helpful for the decisions which must be taken by conscientious laymen.

Types of Punishment and Their Evaluation

Retributive Punishment

"The eye for an eye and tooth for a tooth" formula for punishment, sometimes with exorbitant interest, is probably as old as men, if not older. There is a primitive suggestion of justice here, and the ego satisfaction of having paid back one's assailant in kind. But there are two conclusive objections to it. It doubles the harm done and tends to lead to a war of all against all in which, as Hobbes suggested, life would be ". . . nasty, brutish, and short."

Deterrent Punishment

In one form this directly involves only the offender. Sequestrating him in a prison may keep him from commiting further offenses of the same sort for the duration of his term. But often he emerges a worse, rather than a better man, either soured and embittered against his guards, and against society in general as well and determined to get even, or reduced to a "Milquetoast" shadow of his former self.

Imprisonment or other punishment of a guilty person is also thought to be a deterrent to others and thus to be useful *"pour encourager les autres,"* as the French phrase puts it. Figures on this would surely be hard to obtain, but it seems unlikely that most of those who plan a crime believe themselves incapable of outwitting the law. A quite different but strong reason for not stiffening the punishment of one man in order to deter other and unknown potential doers of a similar deed is that to use the former "merely as a means" is to violate one form of the Categorical Imperative as well as one form of the Golden Rule. Most of us believe that to break either of these moral principles is itself immoral.

Reparational Punishment

Where a criminal act has caused damage primarily to property rather than to persons, it would seem reasonable to sentence the offender to reparations which would be within his ability to pay over a reasonable length of time. Such a punishment should be especially useful in the case of juvenile offenders, where it could be specified that the funds for such reparation payments must be earned by the juvenile through regular commercial or industrial employment. Such a punishment might well help considerably in developing a healthy respect for other people's property.

Reparational punishment seems appropriate in many cases for adults also. It is already used for income tax evaders. Presumably, it could also be used for other monetary crimes, *e.g.,* small ones like shoplifting, or large ones like defrauding a union or a corporation. The rate of payment can be adjusted to suit the ability of the offender to pay.

Treatment, Not Punishment

In what has preceded, I have used the traditional term "punishment." But, if my account of punishment early in this paper is not completely off the mark, it does not stand for the basic concept that we, with our purposes, require. Punishment involves the infliction of harm on the offenders. It is normally justified, if at all, because of past misdeeds. But these deeds have already been done and no punishment can undo them. The only effects we can now bring about must occur in the future. What we want to do is to make the future better than the past, to change our present criminal into a desirable member of our community. Should we not, therefore, regard him as an unfortunate being who, from one cause or another, has become a criminal? He may have contributed to this undesirable development himself but, if so, this was because of the circumstances and experiences which had shaped his life, and his reactions to them. These are all in the past and we cannot retroactively change them. The only thing on which we can have some effect is his future. This we can influence to a considerable degree.

All this suggests that a convict needs treatment. He is genuinely ill, perhaps physically, almost certainly mentally and psychiatrically. He is truly a sick man. He needs help. Something has gone wrong which leads him to react in an antisocial way in situations which stimulate others to constructive actions.

Even those of us who are not physicians, psychologists, psychiatrists or endocrine specialists, and so on, can make a number of relevant distinctions in trying to uncover the causal factors back of, for example, a particular theft. "What was stolen?" we inquire. "A bottle of milk." We ask at once, "Is the thief undernourished, poverty stricken, a child?" But perhaps we get this answer: "He stole a convertible." Then a different type of question is in order. "What possessed him? Was he trying to achieve status? Was he trying to impress a girl?" Or, "Did he steal the convertible for a quick resale to fill his pockets with ready money?"

Or consider a murder committed by a middle-aged man. "What was his motive? Was he trying to silence a blackmailer? Was his act a backlash at a shrewish wife? Did he hope to benefit from Uncle Charlie's estate? Were there physical causes—alcoholism, perhaps, or drug addiction?"

Suppose a respectable member of the community refuses to pay any part of his income tax. We ask: "Is he a pacifist? A miser? An anarchist? A religious fanatic?"

These are questions any reasonable person might raise. They are relevant enough to suggest several competing hypotheses to explain a given person's criminal act. They are not the queries of a specialist. But if specialists were conducting the investigation they would have far more relevant questions to raise. If they can find out what causal factors brought person *A* to commit crime *B* under circumstances *C*, they are well on their way toward prescribing for the offender and/or his situation. As our skilled teams of diagnosticians raise more sophisticated queries, they will, with increasing frequency, be able to specify the principal causal factors responsible for the crime. Once these become known, this knowledge can then be passed on to the experts on proper treatment for the conditions discovered. Then, with time and skill, the offender can be cured and restored to a useful and happy life.

Obviously, a program calling for highly-trained diagnosticians and experts specially skilled in treating and giving professional individual care to prisoners who need it, will be an expensive one. Add to this the diagnosis and care needed by more run-of-the-mill people who are addicted to crime, and the cost will be even greater. Today, no country is willing to adopt such a program. But if we are to do our duty to our fellow human beings, we must take more steps in this direction and as rapidly as possible. If we could learn to avoid the enormous wastes of war, we might be able to turn some of that money, brain-power and scientific knowledge to the life-saving operation of treating law breakers (rather than inflicting retributive punishment upon them) and reap at the same time the vast values of lasting peace.

Good King Pausole's *Code de Tryphême* is reported as having only two articles:

> *I. Ne nuis pas à ton voisin,*
> *II. Ceci bien compris, fais ce qu' il te plait.*

It is rumored he later added:

> *III. Il faut aussi faire du bien.*

References

1. HART, H. L. A.: *The Morality of the Criminal Law*. London, Oxford U. P., 1965, p. 6.
2. WOOTTON, B.: *Social Science and Social Pathology*. London, 1959. Note especially Chap. VIII, Mental disorder and the problem of moral and criminal responsibility.
3. HART, *op. cit.*, p. 14.
4. *Ibid.*, p. 27.
5. *Ibid.*, p. 29.
6. *Ibid.*, p. 26.
7. HART, H. L. A.: *Law, Liberty and Morality*. London, Oxford U. P., 1963. The Henry Camp Lectures, delivered at Stanford University in 1962.
8. MILL, J. S.: *On Liberty*. Chap. 1.
9. HART, *Law, Liberty and Morality*, p. 7.
10. *Ibid.*, p. 10.
11. *Ibid.*, p. 12.
12. *Report of the Committee on Homosexual Offenses and Prostitution*. London, Her Majesty's Stationery Office, 1957, Sec. 61.
13. *Ibid.*
14. HART, *Law, Liberty and Morality*, p. 15.
15. *Ibid.*, p. 22.

PROFESSOR BAYLIS AND THE CONCEPT OF TREATMENT

RICHARD A. KOEHL

I should like to remark at the outset that if I am critical of some of Professor Baylis' ideas in what follows, I will nevertheless be expressing views and delimiting issues in ways which are quite dependent upon the foundations he has laid in his very excellent presentation.

In his paper, Professor Baylis has shown that if punishment has a place in any universe, it has a place in a *deterministic* one. He has shown that even in a deterministic universe there can be freedom of choice, action, and rational motivation; hence, that it can make sense to try to control one's own actions, inclinations, and habits, and to try to get other people to try to control theirs. Having shown this, he has questioned the wisdom of using the power of the state to punish for the sake of morality, as distinguished from punishing for the sake of controlling those actions, inclinations, or habits, the exercise of which would be criminal. This distinction depends, tacitly at least, upon the criterion that what harms others may properly be prosecuted, while that which affects only one's self or affects others only through their consent, is, at worst, immoral. He has argued, quite rightly I think, that the reasons against using the powers of the state to punish for the sake of morality far outweigh any reasons which may be mustered *for* so using that power.

He has then considered three varieties of punishment: retributive, deterrent, and reparational. First, he has argued that retributive punishment, if carried to its logical conclusion, would lead to a Hobbesian war of all against all. Second, he maintains that deterrent punishment is at best immoral in practice, and that only reparational punishment might have a place in an ideally civilized society. Finally, he has suggested that perhaps we ought to strive to attain a society in which the punishment of a citizen by society is replaced by treatment.

In the first part of his paper Professor Baylis put the "freedom-determinism" issue in a perspective which goes far in clarifying the whole family of problems to which the concepts of freedom and determinism are central; therefore I shall not further concern myself with it.

I agree essentially with the conclusions of the second part of his paper, namely, that we ought to punish adults, if at all, only for criminal acts. I should only like to suggest that the criterion offered for distinguishing between punishing for the sake of morality and punishing criminal acts seems to be inadequate to the task. The notions of "actions which affect only one's self" and "actions which affect others" would seem to cry out for analysis. Those who champion the practice of punishing for the sake of morality might well rejoin to Professor Baylis that there are no actions which affect only one's self—that really, whether it be directly or most circuitously, every action and even every good or evil thought affects at least those one loves and those with whom one has relationships of mutual dependency. Proponents of such a position might urge this is the true justification of the punishment of adults by society, as well as of the punishment of children by their parents.

In a similar vein, I think there may be difficulties with reparational punishment. Two objections may be raised against it by those who champion retributive and deterrent forms of punishment. First, it is not quite just, since every attempt to make punishment reparational results ultimately in making the degree the guilty one suffers for his guilt inversely proportional to the amount of his wealth: i.e., the poor man suffers much more than the wealthy man in making the identical reparation. Second, it is ineffective in preventing or repairing the effects of large scale crime as opposed to petty crime. The businessman who steals a dollar from each of ten thousand customers is only too happy, when caught, to return a dollar to a single complaining customer.

But these are peripheral matters. My central concern is with Professor Baylis' fourth and last point: the recommendation that punishment be replaced by treatment. I seriously doubt such a proposal is consistent with our conception of human rights.

Professor Baylis makes strong concessions to human rights when he offers the plea that we keep our concepts of sin and crime distinct; and again, when he endorses Mill's principle that we should not punish adults in the name of their own good. He seems to lose

sight of them, at least temporarily, when his analysis becomes preoccupied with the possibility that we may come to scientifically
understand the causal genesis of criminal acts, and thereby put
ourselves collectively in a position to treat rather than punish
criminal offenders.

There is, of course, an appearance of improvement between
the two situations when in our mind's eye we first see a man rotting
in jail for the alleged good of deterring others, then see him being
treated, cured and released. But I submit that the appearance of
improvement presented to us by such a thought-experiment is a
delusion into which we are seduced by the suggestive analogy with
medical treatment and the concomitant subsumption of criminal
behavior under the category of disease. While we very probably
can differentiate motives in ways similar to those Professor Baylis
has outlined, there is no evidence that all or even most criminals
are neurotic or psychotic. Nor, apart from the special cases of
drug addiction and kleptomania, is there any evidence that curing
sufferers of mental disease cuts the incidence of crime. Giving
psychotherapy to criminals might result in making them more
effective criminals. Professor Baylis' position is reminiscent of the
Socratic belief that no one knowingly does anything except what
is best, but with this apparent difference: Baylis' version seems
to hold that no mentally healthy person ever knowingly breaks
the law. That someone has broken the law then becomes the
justification, not for punishing him, but for treating him for his
mental aberration. Baylis suggests that if we look to the genesis
of criminal acts we can discover the literal and symbolic reasons
the offender had for acting as he did. Presumably, criminal acts
sometimes turn out to be cases where the criminal unknowingly
opted for an alternative lower in the rewards scale than another
which was open to him in reality, so the cure for him will be re-
education. In other cases, criminal acts will turn out to be motivated by symbolic misperceptions of reality. In these cases,
therapy of some kind would be in order. But at the risk of seeming
pessimistic in the face of this optimism, I fear we have by this
turn quite eroded our originally sacrosanct distinction between sin
and crime. For what, at this turn, are we treating? Have we not
replaced the punishment of improper actions by the treatment of

improper motives, and is not the distinction between thought and action (the distinction between lust and rape for example) central to that between sin and crime? Further, need we not remind ourselves that Socrates' confidence rested on his faith that the Eternal Forms could provide measures and standards no rational man could reject? Apart from such standards, it is difficult to see how Baylis' program could be carried out without violation of human rights.

There is no objective standard of mental health available to serve as the measure against which behavior may be identified as deviant or normal. Mental health is a normative concept. To appeal to it as what is best may be to ignore Mill's principle. Common sense allows that for the patient's good it is permissable for the physician to cauterize, to puncture, and to lance, for the sake of health. But we may not on that account overlook the enormous difference between voluntary and involuntary submission to treatment. Indeed, one wonders whether it is proper to call "treatment" the interference with the body or the psyche of a prisoner, if it is imposed upon him without his consent and cooperation. To banish punishment from the universe only to replace it with treatment imposed upon prisoners without their consent, or worse, to exact from prisoners a form of consent to such procedures and a show of cooperation in them as a condition of eventual release, would be, I strongly fear, to banish punishment in name only and to give to it new and more insidious forms.

DISCUSSION OF "IMMORALITY, CRIME, AND TREATMENT"

Peter F. Regan

Professor Baylis' paper is indeed an admirable one, and most of its points are covered with such clarity and elegance that I shall forego discussion of them at this time. The focus of this discussion will be the issue of "treatment, not punishment" in the hope that our symposium may resolve some paradoxes which appear therein.

Like Professor Baylis, I must begin with the individual in the paradigm situation which includes punisher and punishee. I believe, however, a more complete picture may be seen by turning our attention to the punishee, rather than to the punisher.

When we examine punishment with the punishee in mind, the picture of punishment becomes larger and, I think, different. Punishment is one of many phenomena which may follow an action an individual performs.

All of our social experience in life assures us that acts are followed by consequences: good ones, bad ones, or a mixture of both. In fact, this is how we learn to live in society, ". . . to think reasonably and . . . act rationally." We learn from our earliest years that certain acts bring rewards and other acts bring punishment. We learn to guide our activities in the face of these realities of life.

Certainly this is a larger concept of punishment than that proposed by Professor Baylis. It is different, however, only in that it recognizes two forms of punishment:

Informal punishment, which is meted out spontaneously by individuals and groups in response to behavior considered deviant.

Institutionalized punishment, which is meted out in accordance with legal and penal codes, or other devices, in response to deviant behavior.

Both of these punishment types rest on the same base. They are expressions of the value system used by a society (large or small). If a society dislikes noise, or private property, or nudity— or if it likes them—it will establish rewards and punishments which reflect its values. Some of these values, in turn, will be regarded as so important that they will become embodied in legal and penal codes; some will not. Both kinds of values, however, will find expression in reward and punishment.

Now, it is clear that values differ from society to society, and from age to age. It is also clear that institutionalization of values can bring about warping and lag, i.e., the institutionalized values may not accurately reflect basic values to begin with, and the two may grow farther apart as society changes and codes remain static. Certainly the thinking social man is always justified, both in attempting to change his society's values, and also in striving to make its institutionalized codes congruent with its real values. In this light, I am completely sympathetic to Professor Baylis' manifest desires for reform in such areas as homosexuality, although

I suspect that other students would single out values relating to war, economic policy, international trade etc., as being equally in need of change.

I must confess, however, to apprehension regarding Professor Baylis' extension of his argument to a position which eliminates punishment (at least in its institutional aspects) in favor of treatment. Even at a general level, the implications of this position are staggering. The legal and penal codes may certainly possess vagaries and brutalities, but they *do* reflect a society's values, however imperfectly. It is important, moreover, to recognize their purpose. They are intended to protect the individual from the far more unpredictable and ferocious punishments that society metes out when its values are not institutionalized. If the codes do not punish, the vigilantes and the vendetta will. At a general level, I would hope that we might fight for more intelligent and appropriate codes, and not for a return to the law of the jungle.

These considerations cause even more concern when we view them in the light of the individual punishee. Let us remember two key points:

> *The individual lives in a society* which does have values, and does reward and punish, in both formal and informal fashions. *The healthy individual* has learned to live his life by recognizing these signposts. When he chooses to act in opposition to the values, he may do so either in the hope of not being caught, or in the conviction that the gain is worth the punishment.

What of the sick person? Without becoming deeply involved in psychopathology, let us recognize two types of mental illness: that which disrupts a person's grasp of reality, and that which interferes with his ability to deal with the real world in a sound fashion. Parenthetically, the latter condition is most frequently attributed to the absence of a society-oriented system of reward and punishment during the formative years.

Certainly, such sick people deserve treatment when they act in opposition to society's values. The purpose of treatment, however, is to help them be able to grasp reality, to obtain rewards and avoid punishments as independent beings. In many ways, psychotherapeutic treatment resembles an education in reward and punishment.

In this context, it is evident that a world in which treatment is substituted for punishment virtually eliminates rational treatment: first, because such a world cannot exist in reality; second, because without reward and punishment, treatment cannot be pursued.

Let me close by pointing to one individual: myself.

Today, your planning committee has granted me the privilege of standing on this platform and addressing you. All of my experience informs me that my actions will be rewarded or punished. I know this, and each of you knows this.

If I do well, reward will come from approbation, respect, friendship.

If I do poorly by virtue of laziness or incompetence, disapprobation will punish me; I will be chastized for laziness, or taught better to recognize my limits.

If I do poorly through ignorance of your society's values, disapprobation will punish me; with the help of friends, I can be better prepared on future occasions.

If I deliberately antagonize, insult, slander, or incite to riot, my punishment may be much more severe; presumably, I will have done so in the conviction that the gain is worth the punishment.

But suppose none of these conditions prevail. Suppose I cannot recognize that reward or punishment will follow my acts. Suppose I flout your values, and cannot recognize the punishment you inflict.

Such obliviousness to the possiblity of, or expression of, punishment would cause you to consider me mentally ill. Having been judged ill, I hope some friend would arrange for me to receive treatment. How would the treatment proceed, if it were based on the notion that punishment does not exist?

REPLY TO COMMENTATORS

Charles A. Baylis

Thank you for your kind words about my paper, but even more thanks for your critical comments. I appreciate especially your questions and misgivings about my views on, first, the relationship between sin, immorality and crime; and, second, the overlap between punishment and treatment.

The Relationship Between Sin, Immorality and Crime

To sin is to act contrary to our religious beliefs. But there are
many religions in the world, the precepts of each being in varying
respects incompatible with those of any other. We who accept
a common set of religious beliefs are committed to acting in
accordance with them. But the same is true of those who accept
religious beliefs incompatible with ours. If we believe in religious
freedom, as I do, we are convinced we should not force our
religious beliefs and practices on those who do not share our
faith. And certainly, we should not invoke the powers of the
state to enforce conformity on them.

The situation is similar with conflicting moral beliefs. We cannot
conscientiously obey the moral beliefs of others whose beliefs are
incompatible with our own. Each of us must, if he is sincere, act
in accordance with the moral principles he himself holds. But
this is equally true of those who accept principles in conflict with
ours. To act otherwise is, we believe, immoral. But to claim
for ourselves this freedom to act in accordance with our moral
beliefs entails granting a similar right to those who conscientiously
differ from us. The reasons for rejecting state-enforced punishment for those who act in accordance with moral principles different from our own parallel those which permit acting in accordance with different religious principles. Detailed reasons against
making such acts "crimes" are presented in the last paragraphs
in the section on "Crime and Immorality" in my paper. As in
the case of acts consequent upon religious beliefs different from
our own, the only justification for punishing them would be that
to allow these acts would, in all probability, result in considerably
greater harm than the obvious evils which would follow from destroying or undermining the well-established habits of obeying
cherished principles. Cases of this type are very rare.

The Overlap Between Punishment and Treatment

Both of my critics properly call attention to the fact that there is
seldom, if ever, a complete dichotomy between treatment and
punishment. The heading of "Treatment, Not Punishment" in my
paper is an overstatement. To this I must, perforce, agree. To
treat criminals therapeutically involves at a minimum some de-

terrence and confinement, and often some pain and suffering, mental as well as physical. Rare indeed is the person who likes to have his habits of attitude or action altered. Being forced to learn new modes of behavior, better though they may be, is often painful. Educational, sociological and psychiatric therapy are not at all as advanced as medical knowledge and therapy.

With all this I quite agree. Nevertheless the import of the terms "punishment" and "treatment" are very different. The former suggests retribution and implies the deliberate infliction of suffering. The latter aims at reform and rehabilitation, using deterrence and pain only as it is needed to bring those goals to realization. To be sure, the threat of punishment is itself often regarded as a deterrent and as an inhibitor of antisocial behavior. But statistics seem to indicate that it is a very poor one. Treatment which changes the antisocial habits and goals of a person to socially desirable ones, though difficult, seems much more likely to bring about the desired increase in socially acceptable behavior.

One of my critics expresses serious doubts about the rightness of tinkering with the minds (or souls) of criminals whose motives must indeed be changed if their social behavior is to become acceptable. I agree we should proceed with caution here. However, medical men have already developed an acceptable procedure, much of which is adaptable to psychiatric treatment: They experiment with animals before testing their procedures on humans. In the case of dangerous operations, they explain the risks both of operating and of not operating, of one treatment as contrasted with another, and they accept the decision of the patient or of someone qualified to speak for him. Only when time is of the essence, where seconds count, and where only one course of action offers any reasonable hope, do they proceed without delay.

There seems to be no clear reason why mental treatment cannot follow analogous principles. Experimentation with animals can precede treatment of humans. In the case of psychiatric treatment the alternative risks involved can be made clear to the prisoner-patient and he can be given his choice. If he cannot give assent himself, it can be requested of someone who can speak for him. Only in emergencies, where immediate action is imperative, and where the alternatives are either death or grievous insanity on the one hand and a possibly much better life on the other, is dangerous treatment without consent justifiable. But in such cases it is.

Finally, the whole motivational picture of punishment is very different from that which underlies treatment. The goal of the latter is the cure, or at least the alleviation of tendencies toward antisocial behavior. The goal of the former is to obtain social conformity through threats of suffering or inflicted suffering. A prisoner facing punishment can hardly avoid picturing as sadists those who order it or carry it out. By contrast, a prisoner awaiting treatment can learn to expect friendly guidance and professional help.

RETRIBUTION REVISITED

BRAND BLANSHARD

P UNISHMENT is unpleasant to inflict and not particularly pleasant to discuss. But we clearly need to discuss it. Whatever else it may be, punishment is commonly supposed to be a deterrent of crime, and the Federal Bureau of Investigation tells us crime has been increasing about five times as fast as our population. In one recent year, it informs us, there were 8,027 murders; 12,886 rapes by force; 66,843 robberies; 110,672 aggravated assaults; 603,707 burglaries, and 265,179 automobiles stolen. In the following year, these crimes increased by 9.3 per cent to the point where there was a serious crime for every 111 persons in the population. An 8 per cent rise has been reported for the first half of this year (1966). Clearly our present system of apprehending and punishing criminals is in need of review.

A remark or two on this situation may perhaps be hazarded before I turn to my own special aspect of the problem. No improvement in our modes of punishment will by itself cure this epidemic disease. Punishment may retard the spread of crime, but it cannot get at its root. That root lies in inward attitudes— in a lack of regard for others, in disrespect for their rights, in selfishness and self-pity, in confusion and thoughtlessness. This is the sort of thoughtlessness, for example, which claims a privilege for oneself that one would not dream of granting to others, or considers law and government and police not as extensions of oneself, but as hostile and repressive forces. Punishment, even if repeated and severe, may leave these roots untouched. I recall a report in *The New York Times* of a man who was currently serving his 205th jail term. It has often been pointed out that in days when boys in their teens were hanged for picking pockets, the picking of pockets still went on in the crowds assembled to view the hangings. The only effective cure for pocket-picking lies in a change of thought and feeling about it. If a person thinks it is a clever and proper thing to do, even the threat of the gallows may not stop him, and every additional punishment is evidence that the punishment has failed. On the other hand, if he comes to think of picking pockets as a really contemptible thing to do, the chances are that he will avoid it, whether threatened or not. The root of criminal conduct lies in defects of attitude and character, and these defects are rooted not in the weakness of our system of punishment, but in failures in education and the home.

It is often said these latter defects have their roots in a still deeper stratum. Why the failures in school and home? Most of them occur, we are told, in poverty-stricken areas—in Watts and Harlem, in the Brooklyn and Chicago slums. The deepest roots of crime are economic: lack of money, lack of jobs, lack of assurance about holding a job, even if one has it. This account of the matter, popular on the extreme left, is not to be dismissed as irrelevant; it *is* relevant, and it surely does give a partial explanation. The trouble with it, however, is that it is so very partial in both senses of the word. Granting that proverty often contributes to crime, we must also add that many admirable characters have wormed their way up through heavy blankets of it, while many who have never known it have gone on to become ". . . malefactors of great wealth." In short, there is no firm linkage between poverty and crime. Let us do what we can by all means to get rid of poverty, but let us remember, too, that to eliminate crime we must cleanse the inside as well as the outside of the cup.

Two Traditions of Punishment

The causes of crime and legal procedures for dealing with it are food for the sociologist, the criminologist and the lawyer. I cannot qualify in any of these capacities. Such limited competence as I have lies in ethics, and my interest lies in this question: Why should we punish at all, either the criminal who takes a life, or the small boy who takes his sister's lollipop? Now if you ask for the grounds on which men have justified themselves in punishing others, you get a wide diversity of answers. Sometimes they say their victim deserves it; sometimes, that they must teach him not to do it again; sometimes, that they must use him as an example to deter others; sometimes that punishment is needed to channel the explosive force of revenge; sometimes, that it is needed to bring home to the victim how bad his behavior is; sometimes, that it is needed as a quarantine to protect the public against him; sometimes, as in the case of witches, that it is a divine command.

These answers are not as different as they seem. If we look below the surface, we shall find all of them falling into one of two types:

First, punishment is to be given either because a man is morally bad and such punishment is the appropriate requital. Or second, because it is a necessary means to future good.

It is not surprising that these should be the two ultimate grounds proposed for punishment, for they reflect the two chief ways of settling any ethical problem. On the one hand are the moralists like Kant, Prichard, and Ross, who hold that there is, or may be, something in the character of the act itself (as distinct from anything it leads to) which makes it right or wrong. On the other hand, there are those who, like Aristotle, Sidgwick, and Moore, believe we should always act in order to produce the greatest good. It is natural for those who hold the first view to say that the treatment of a wicked man should be suited to the character of his acts, and for those who hold the second view to say that, even here, we should suit our treatment of him to his own good and that of the community. Behind men's differences over punishment is this fundamental difference over what makes any action right. It will conduce to clarity if I state at once where I stand on this ultimate issue. I must risk the sound of dogmatism in doing so, since there is no time to argue the matter out; I have tried to do that elsewhere.

Of these two ethical traditions, I belong to the second. For me the major rule, the great rule of conduct—the only rule without exceptions—is that we should so act as to produce the greatest good, not only our own good, but that of all who are affected by our action. So far, this is utilitarianism. But the traditional teaching of that school must be modified, I think, in two ways.

First, the good which tests the act cannot be limited to that of the act taken in isolation. Prichard and Ross have shown that it is sometimes a duty to keep a promise or repay a debt even when the greater good would seem to be produced by breaking our engagement. If I have agreed to repay a loan on a certain day, I ought to repay it instead of giving the money to a relief agency, even though the latter would use it to better advantage than my creditor. If we are to defend repayment on the grounds of its greater good, this good must be that entailed not by the act taken in isolation, but by the complex of rules with which this one is bound up, or, as Joseph would put it, by the form of life to which this rule belongs. Difficult questions plainly arise here, which ought, if there were time, to be dealt with; I can only say that they do not seem to me unanswerable.

Second, what sort of consequences are relevant? Not pleasures and pains solely, as utilitarians hold, but experiences of any kind having value or disvalue. What gives an experience intrinsic value? Two things, I think. First, it must fulfill some drive, demand or impulse of human nature. Food is intrinsically good only to the hungry man, knowledge to the curious man, music to the man with a musical ear and interest. Secondly, the fulfillment must bring with it some complement of pleasure. If eating, learning and listening to music brought with them no pleasure at all, they would have no intrinsic value, however great their value as means to an end. My categorical imperative, then, is this: Choose that action—or, more strictly, that network of cognate actions—which will produce for those affected by it the greatest fulfillment and happiness.

The Retributiveness of Common Sense

If there is any sphere in which the view of the ordinary man runs counter to this principle, it is in the sphere of punishment. Most ordinary men, I think, would accept a retributive theory, though not quite consistently, as we shall see. Here, retribution means the infliction of suffering on a guilty man because of his guilt and in proportion to it. This theory has played an immense part in people's half-conscious thought and action, and still does. I propose to devote this paper to reviewing and criticizing it.

We should say that if a man steps on another man's foot because he is pushed in a crowd, no guilt attaches to causing the injury, and it would be absurd to punish him. If he leaves his car on an incline so that it rolls away and hits another's car, we think he should make reparation, but we should also feel this is enough. He was careless in not tightening his brake, but the guilt of that hardly seems worth punishing. If he produces the same damage by deliberately ramming another man's car, we should say that reparation alone would not be enough; this is wrong-doing of a serious kind and should be punished sternly. If he deliberately runs a pedestrian down, this is a sort of wickedness which must be punished most severely, and if, in so doing, he kills the man, nothing but the most severe penalty—his life or life imprisonment—seems to fit the blackness of his guilt. Many of us can remember how we felt when we read in the newspaper a few years ago that a respected Kansas family had been savagely wiped out one night by a pair of hoodlums in search of money and excitement. Mr. Capote's vivid account of the crime and its sequel has had many readers. I suppose one of their chief satis-factions has been in following and cheering the district attorney for running the villains to ground and bringing them to what was felt to be a just accounting on the gallows.

Many of us can go back farther and recall our reactions to the news of what had gone on at Auschwitz and Dachau. I do not think our state of mind was one of fear that genocide might recur, or of reflection on the steps required to prevent this; we could hardly believe such things had happened even once. Our feeling was, rather, one of horrified anger and of hope that the monsters responsible for these things would be ferreted out and given what they deserved. In the first essay of his *Ethical Studies,* F. H. Bradley undertook to summarize the ordinary man's view on punishment, which was apparently also his own:

> If there is any opinion to which the man of uncultivated morals is attached, it is the belief in the necessary connection of punishment and guilt. Punishment is punishment only where it is deserved. We pay the penalty because we owe it, and for no other reason; and if punishment is inflicted for any other reason whatever than because it is merited by wrong, it is a gross immorality, a crying injustice, an abominable crime, and not what it pretends to be.[1]

Now the average man's judgment carries some weight even on speculative questions. Common sense is itself a kind of philosophy;

it has a long experience behind it, and anyone who dissents from it should accept the burden of proof. But it is certainly not infallible, and I am inclined to think that here it is mistaken. I doubt whether retributive punishment, meaning the infliction of suffering on a man simply by reason of his guilt, is ever justifiable. I admit it is natural for us to think it is; indeed, perhaps the best way to raise doubts about the theory is to see that our nature and history have committed us to it, whether justifiable or not.

The Origin of the Retributive Theory

Some people think of punishment as something worked out as a means for the enforcement of law. The truth is it is far older than law or government. It had its start, no doubt, in instinctive anger. *X* sneered that *Y* was a coward; or he stole *Y's* axe or canoe; or worse, he tried to steal *Y's* wife, and *Y* blazed out at him. *Y* might say he was going to teach *X* a lesson, or that if this sort of thing were allowed to go on, it would be a danger to everybody, but these are not the motives that really move him. If the same thing had happened to someone else, he would not have felt it nearly as deeply. He is hurt, he is offended, enraged, and he takes his anger out on its victim directly. This is almost certainly the way punishment began.

That this is in truth its origin is supported by the indiscriminateness of early punishment. Anger is apt to strike out at the offender wildly, blind to all distinctions reflection would introduce. Public concern about serious offenses in early days was largely directed to checking the savagery of avengers rather than to punishing the offenders themselves. The Old Testament cities of refuge were set up ". . . that everyone that killeth any person unawares may flee thither."[2] The implication is that even persons who inadvertently caused the death of another were so cruelly punished by avengers that it was necessary to take formal steps to protect them. Of course, no refuge was provided for the person who took another life deliberately; he was fair game for any avenger. The law not only permitted but ordered that he be blotted out: "The revenger of blood himself shall slay the murderer; when he meeteth him, he shall slay him."[3]

Where anger takes control, it may break through the most carefully contrived rational harness. Following association rather than reason, it tends to vent itself on anybody or anything connected with the offender. This is just what we find reported in accounts of early punishment. The unfortunate Achan took more than his share of the spoils of Jericho; Joshua's anger with him exploded in all directions; not only Achan, but ". . . his sons, and his daughters, and his oxen, and his asses, and his sheep, and his tent, and all that he had . . ." were first stoned and then burned[4].

This gives us a glimpse into the origin of blood feuds. *X* is inadvertently or deliberately killed by *Y;* *X's* family and friends are enraged, and they go after *Y;* *Y* knows what is coming and hides. They therefore vent their rage on the next best thing to *Y,* a son or brother through whom they can certainly hurt him. This in turn enrages all *Y's* friends, who return the compliment on any of *X's* relatives they can find. Now underway is a full-fledged feud, which may last for generations. When the families or clans involved could support it no longer, and met to halt the slaughter by agreement, they often found it expedient to anticipate and allow for the indiscriminateness of vengeance. Sometimes they protected themselves against the ultimate anger by turning over the culprit while there was yet time. "Thus among the Topanaz, if a man killed a tribesman, accidentally or not, his kinsmen take him to those of the slain man, who strangle him. The two parties then eat together and the affair is settled."[5] Anglo-Saxon law, under some circumstances, allowed a man who was the victim of theft to enslave the family of the man who had stolen from him; and if a thane was killed, his family had a right to demand the lives of six "churls" as his price. Illustrations from primitive practice of this indiscriminateness in primitive vengeance could be extended almost indefinitely. Its extreme is perhaps reached in the practice of some Papuans; if a man's wife is stolen, he is allowed to go into the bush to kill the first man he meets. The custom has proved an effective recipe for perpetual war.

Law and Retribution

When law makes its first tentative efforts to take over the

business of punishment, it raises no question about the legitimacy of retaliation or vengeance; it merely tries to keep the explosive force in channels. If X has injured Y, it is inevitable and right that Y should try to get back at him; but in doing so, let him satisfy himself with hurting X in the same way and degree that X has hurt him. The earliest law laid down in the Old Testament is, "He that sheddeth man's blood, by man shall his blood be shed," and the most familiar example of the law of talion is the prescription of an eye for an eye and a tooth for a tooth, with the grim addendum—not always noted—of ". . . a son for a son, daughter for daughter, slave for slave, ox for ox." Something like this had appeared much earlier in the code of Hammurabi, king of Babylon, in which there is a provision that if a house-builder has built a house for another man, but built it badly so that it collapses and kills the man's son, the builder shall be punished by having his own son put to death.

Law is of little use unless it is enforcible, and if it is to be enforcible, it must not be too far in advance of general morals. To have popular support it needs to reflect rather faithfully how people actually think and feel about crime. And the framing of law at every stage of its history seems to have reflected a retributive attitude in the public mind. Sir Henry Maine, writing about ancient law, says it was formulated partly with public anger in mind. Sir James Stephen, writing of the nineteenth century, says: ". . . the criminal law regulates, sanctions, and provides a legitimate satisfaction for the passion of revenge; the criminal law stands to the passion of revenge in much the same relation as marriage to the sexual appetite." To the extent that this is true, it throws light not only on some anomalies of the law, but also on the human nature the law reflects. Rashdall points out that Roman law "punished the thief caught redhanded twice as severely as the thief convicted afterwards by evidence taken in cold blood."[6] A man who tries unsuccessfully to kill another is on the same ethical level as if he had succeeded, but he is not treated in the same way. In fact, magistrates have been known to postpone decision on a prisoner until it is learned whether his victim is going to get well or not. The law in such cases reflects the difference in public indignation toward a murder as against a mere attempt at it. Again, though murder has been committed by many women in this country, very few have ever paid the extreme penalty for it. Only rarely can judges and juries feel the same way toward a woman as they do toward a man who has committed a crime of passion.

Religion and Retribution

Vindictiveness would seem to be an un-Christian way of feeling, and it may be asked whether religion has not served to assuage vindictive punishment. To show that it has served nobly at times to soften the ferocities of punishment, one need only mention such names as Pope Clement XI, William Penn and Elizabeth Fry. But looked at in larger perspective, the influence of religion has been ambiguous. The God of the Old Testament gave no very convincing example to his people of either forgiveness or justice; he was a jealous and angry God, easy to wrath and implacable in his vengeance. If Joshua wished to stone Achan, or Samuel to hew Agag in pieces before an altar, it was easy to claim divine sanction for it. I have on my shelves a book by Canon E. B. Pusey, which brings all the learning of a Regius Professor at Oxford to show there is no escape from the doctrine of hell, that even the God of the New Testament, together with the saints and fathers of the early church, was committed to punishing much of the human race eternally. There is, unhappily, no doubt that the impulse to sadistic extremes of retribution has often been fortified by religion. Thousands of miserable women have been put to death as witches under cover of the Biblical injunction. "Thou shalt not suffer a witch to live"; and with the support of Pope Innocent III, the Albigenses were punished for heresy by being hunted down and exterminated with all their works, so that no one to this day knows much about them. Luther's attitude toward the peasant's revolt, Calvin's toward Servetus, and the attitude of the Deity they worshipped toward mankind, were not so far in advance of this practice as one could desire. And if much cruelty in the past has been based on alleged divine command, much also has been based on the attempt to escape the terrors of divine retribution. The sacrifices of children at Carthage, and of youths and maidens among the Aztecs were not, of course, attempts to punish anyone. They were attempts to turn the edge of "the terrible swift sword" that threatened from above, to appease by extreme sacrifice an anger that could blight the whole people. In the Gilgamesh epic of the Babylonians, written some twenty centuries before Christ, there is already an appeal to the god to destroy the sinner rather than turn his anger to destroying mankind. Man's anxious imagination has projected upon the skies gods who reflected their own belief in vengeance and fortified it.

Freedom and Retribution

This belief has been confirmed again by men's confidence in their freedom of choice. They have felt no serious doubt that at a given moment they were facing genuine alternatives in conduct, with nothing forcing them to one course or another. When they look back at a lie they told yesterday, they are sure they could have told the truth instead; this, they would say, is why they feel remorse about it. If they were not free, if they were like the insane man who cannot help doing what he does, no one could ever be called wicked, however disastrous his actions. Mary Lamb, who was a gentle soul like her famous brother, killed her mother with a kitchen knife. Was she therefore a murderess? Her friends knew she was not, they knew that blame would only intensify her misery, and that what she needed was commiseration and a hospital. So it is of other people. If they are really puppets, pulled about by physiological or Freudian wires, we should limit ourselves to manipulating them as best we can in the public interest. But it is self-evident we are not such puppets ourselves, and there is no reason to suppose that other people are. When a normal man chooses to do wrong, he turns down an opportunity (which was equally open to him) of doing right. Anyone who does this is morally guilty; indeed, that is what guilt means. And guilt deserves to be punished; is not that, too, self-evident? Of course, this would make us all deserve punishment: ". . . use every man after his desert, and who should 'scape whipping?" Still, it is not very practicable to administer a daily whipping to everyone, and since there are big and little sins, it seems prudent to reserve punishment for the big ones. In the ordinary man's mind, punishment rests on guilt, and guilt rests on freedom.

The Pleasure of Hating

If we are to understand the grasp of the retributive theory on the ordinary mind, we must add a reference to certain ugly facts celebrated by Hazlitt in his essay on "The Pleasure of Hating." Revenge is sweet and men enjoy inflicting it.

> . . . without something to hate [Hazlitt says, and, like Johnson, he was 'a good hater'] we should lose the very spring of thought and action. . . . Do we not see this principle at work everywhere? Animals torment and worry one another without mercy; children kill flies for sport: everyone reads the accidents and offences in a newspaper. . . . Men assemble in crowds, with eager enthusiasm, to witness a tragedy: but if there were an execution going forward in the next street, as Mr. Burke observes, the theatre would be left empty.[7]

"I think that there are but two pleasures permitted to mortal man," said Lady Mary Wortley Montague, "love and vengeance." Unfortunately, love is harder to arouse than detestation, and is less likely to remain. Though some inhibition is placed by the social code on the verbal venting of animosity, there is many a small group which is largely dedicated to the skilful dismembering of persons not present. Also, in the privacy of a sleepless night or in a journal, vengeance may be rolled under the tongue with relish. Listen, for example, to this confession by the Duc de St. Simon on hearing that the Duc du Maine had been publicly disgraced:

> "I fairly died of joy; I was afraid of swooning with it; my heart, swelling to excess, had no space to swell more . . . I triumphed; I had my revenge; I enjoyed the complete fulfillment of the most insistent desires of my whole life".[8]

If hatred can rise to this lyrical pitch in a mind acting alone, it is hard to set any limit to it when resonated and intensified by the presence of a lynching mob.

So far we have seen that punishment originates in anger and resentment, that primitive law embodies this resentment along with much of its indiscriminateness, and that the spirit of retribution has been fortified by certain elements in traditional religion, by men's confidence that they are free agents, and by the satisfaction they take in revenge. The psychological forces making for retributive punishment have been and are almost overwhelming.

The Importance of Resentment

Is an attitude so deeply rooted in human nature and, for those who have it, so clearly justified, to be dismissed as immoral? Many sensitive and enlightened persons have insisted, on the contrary, that it is an essential part of the good man's equipment. "Revenge, my friends," said Thomas Carlyle, "revenge and the natural hatred of scoundrels, and the ineradicable tendency to *revancher* oneself upon them, and pay them what they have merited; this is forever intrinsically a correct, and even a divine feeling in the mind of every man."

The discerning critic to whom I have just referred, F. L. Lucas, writes:

> There are wishy-washy people who mask their indolence or coward-ice under intolerable tolerance—the sort of persons who travelled quite serenely in Fascist Italy, and thought the Nazis had their good points, if only the war-mongering liberals would not irritate them. There are times when it is good to be angry; there are things that it is feeble not to loathe . . . there is no place for good humour in front of Belsen and Buchenwald.[9]

Another writer I admire, H. W. Nevinson, went farther:

> A prayer for perfect hatred may seem a strange petition to the holy spirit. Yet, after all, one should always, I suppose, pray for the power most opposite to one's natural weakness, and my natural weakness is tolerance, politeness, moderation, a judicial benevolence or sympathetic understanding toward the atrocious enemy. I can even understand Hitler and feel a stupid tolerance of Mussolini. So I can only repeat the prayer in terrified apprehension . . . lest it might be said of me, as many years ago I said of a certain rising politician:
>
> > Peace, mercy, justice, resolution brave,
> > Love for mankind and freedom—all are gone
> > And now his soul lies mouldering in the grave
> > And his body goes marching on.[10]

Certainly the call to a "wide and capable revenge" has often seemed just at the time, and indeed justified in retrospect as well. To many persons, Voltaire has been the very image of a cackling, overcerebral, irresponsible cynic, but when he read the news that Jean Calas, a Protestant merchant, had been broken on the wheel at Toulouse for murdering his son (of which he was innocent)

Voltaire ceased to laugh and cackle. He vowed implacable vengeance, and raised a battlecry, *"Écrasez l'infame!"*, which echoed throughout Europe. As Lecky said:

> Beneath his withering irony persecution appeared not only criminal but loathsome, and since his time it has ever shrunk from observation, and masked its features under other names. He died, leaving a reputation that is indeed far from spotless, but having done more to destroy the greatest of human curses than any other of the sons of men.[11]

His sarcophagus in the Panthéon bears the simple words, *"Il vengea Calas."*

I make no apology for introducing the views of men like Carlyle and Voltaire into a discussion of this kind. They were not great philosophers, but unlike some present-day philosophers, they had strong moral convictions, they did not believe such convictions were emotional spasms merely, and their laughter would have buried the notion that one could settle speculative problems by scrutinizing verbal usage. But the question is still before us whether or not they were right. Is retributory punishment, revenge on a wrongdoer, the infliction on guilty persons of pain or deprivation solely by reason of their guilt, ever morally justifiable?

Concessions to the Retributive Theory

We must grant the retributivists several things. First, the repulsion against moral evil as such is plainly legitimate. It is not enough to recognize evil intellectually; cruelty, for example, is hateful and properly hated, even if causally inevitable. The French murderer Lacenaire, who had taken many lives, said he felt nothing more when he took a human life than when he took the life of a fly. Such a man is probably a congenital moral moron, but whether he can help himself or not, that attitude toward his fellowman is one toward which horror and repulsion are the only appropriate feelings. Suppose we discovered that St. Francis, Michelangelo, and Jack the Ripper were all completely determined in what they did; would this show that love for the saint, honor for the artist, and hatred for the sadist would now have become unfitting? I do not see how it would.

Second, we may grant, with the support of many thoughtful

persons, that anger at wrong-doing, and even the desire for revenge, may be socially useful. One of the most coolheaded of moralists, Henry Sidgwick, said: ". . . if we could suppress the passion for revenge without effecting any other change in the moral nature of average men, we should do more harm than good."[12] The psychologist William McDougall, after pointing out that the adminstration of criminal law is largely "the organized regulated expression of the anger of society" goes on to say: ". . . in the nursery and the school righteous anger will always have a great and proper part to play in the training of the individual for his life in society."[13] Gilbert Murray writes in similar vein: "Punishment is a blessed thing. I pity the young who have grown up without it. I pity the old, the masters and mistresses of households, whom nobody dares to contradict, who are never, never put into the corner or whipped as they deserve."[14] Murray was the most tenderhearted of men; he could never forget the time when, as a boy, he was playing with Rudyard Kipling, young Kipling threw a stone at a cat. He believed, nevertheless, that by sparing the rod one could spoil a child.

Third, we must grant it is not enough to say, Hate the act, but not the man. The act *is* the man. Morally speaking, the act includes the motive, and the motive springs out of the man's character and provides the most accurate index of his quality. Divorce a man's behavior from its inner springs, and it is no more guilty or praiseworthy than a tile that falls from the roof. The tile is not wicked if it hits a man, because it did not mean to; but the man, if he did that, would be wicked because he did mean to. The advice to condemn the deed but not the doer is thus the reverse of the truth. It is the man who is bad, not the play of his arm and leg.

We have said retribution is punishment dealt out as the desert of wrongdoing. There is a fourth element of truth in this view. It is an element that forms the main point of Hegel's theory of punishment, which is often taken as a retributive theory. The object of punishment, Hegel held, is to produce in the sinner himself the attitude most appropriate to his sin, namely, repentance. This is not a reformatory theory if that means that the object of punishment is to prevent the man from repeating the act, nor is it retributive, if that means that the pain is itself the desert of the sin.

The pain is designed to bring home to the sinner the fact that he really has done wrong, to make him see himself as he is, and become aware of the gap between what he is and what he might be, should be, and really wants to be. We do not punish a man as we do a dog, to get future results. Punishment, says Hegel, is ". . . the criminal's right, and hence by being punished he is honored as a rational being."[15] He is presumed to have an interest in knowing and doing what is right, and, therefore, to be capable of even gratitude for a punishment which makes these possible.

Now I do not suppose that anyone, including Hegel, would offer this as an adequate basis for legal punishment. That a stiff jail term would bring Al Capone or Lucky Luciano to his knees in contrition is not a very high probability. If they were hungry for light and accepted the law or current standards as reflecting that light, there would be some hope, but not if they were expressly at war with them. Even McTaggart, who thinks well of the Hegelian theory, admits: ". . . if the state allows its attention to be distracted in the humble task of frightening criminals from crime, by the higher ambition of converting them to virtue, it is likely to fail in both. . . ."[16]

But Hegel is not to be dismissed lightly. I remember the comment of a respected tutor of mine, Harold Joachim, to the effect that though he had found many obscure and forbidding passages in Hegel, he had never found one which did not, after a long or short mental wrestle, yield a rewarding meaning. It is clear on reflection that punishment often does work as Hegel says it should. A boy may know in a vague way that he should not take a toy from the boy next door or tell him an untruth, but he is much more likely to realize the seriousness of theft or untruthfulness if his father punishes him for it. A college student who cheats on an examination may excuse it to himself by saying it is a common practice, but when his paper is torn up and he is failed in the course, he will be less light of heart about dishonesty. From 1776 on, Americans have recited that all men are equal, but by some it has been recited with the lips only, and the threat of a jail sentence has had to be added to make them realize this really does apply to Negroes. No doubt one cannot make men moral by act of Parliament, if it means they will accept as morally binding any law Parliament cares to pass (witness the failure of prohibition). But where men are not aware that something is wrong, or are in doubt about it, or, knowing it is wrong, are inclined to do it anyhow, law and the threat of punishment may very well make them moral in the sense of waking them up to an evil which they never before regarded seriously.

The retributive theory must be granted a fifth and final value. It has sometimes been rejected on the ground that the very attempt to punish moral guilt is absurd. The objectors have a case, as we shall see. But they have sometimes gone on to infer that law and punishment do not have a moral ground at all. That is a mistake. A government cannot, to be sure, directly control men's states of mind; it cannot legislate the sense of duty, or a sense of guilt. But this is not the only way to serve moral ends. These inward states themselves are of value only because they subserve the supreme end of all moral effort: the good of mankind. The ethical end also provides the end of the state and of all its laws and punishments. The insistence upon this has been the virtue of the entire line of political theorists from Rousseau, through Green, to Hobhouse. They held that the state was brought into being as a means to the general good, that every law it passed was a subordinate means to this good, and that every punishment it inflicted was to be judged by its contribution to this good. No other theory of the state seems to me even plausible. My doubts about the retributive theory spring chiefly from the fact that it cannot be made to fit in with a view in ethics and politics that seems to me irresistible. Where exactly does it fall short?

Retribution and Gratuitous Suffering

This theory falls short in four conspicuous ways: first and most obviously, in its commitment to pointless suffering. Some suffering does have point; for example, the suffering inflicted by dentists, parents, surgeons, and Ph.D. committees. It is a necessary means to ends evidently desired by both sufferer and inflicter. But suffering is an intrinsic evil, and we have the right to ask of anyone who imposes it what good he expects to come of it and how he intends to justify its price. Does he impose it to reform the sufferer? The retributionist says, No, that is not what retribution is for. Does he impose it, then, to protect the public through a preventive threat? No, that again would be falling back on consequences. Why then does he impose it? Simply because wickedness deserves suffering. How do you know that? Answer: It is self-evident. Now to anyone inclined, as I am, to hold as self-evident the view that you should produce the largest attainable good, this view that you should add another evil to one which already exists, is not only not self-evident; it seems to conflict with one that is. Indeed, when baldly stated, it seems queer enough to call for an explanation. What explanation is offered?

Sometimes it is this: On reflection we find it fitting, suitable, appropriate, that as good men should be happy, so bad men should be unhappy. But this again is not very convincing. What is really appropriate to the good man is honor and respect, which, to be sure, bring some happiness with them, but not as itself the appropriate tribute. Similarly, what badness calls for is moral condemnation by the offender himself and by others. It is true that this generally gives rise to unhappiness. But the condemnation and the unhappiness are different things, of which it is surely the first that is felt as appropriate rather than the second.

Sometimes the defender of retribution falls back on G. E. Moore's doctrine of organic unities. Moore held pleasure to be a good, and pain an evil. But he held that sometimes the addition of pleasure to a state of mind makes it worse, as in the case of the man who takes pleasure in hatred; and that sometimes the addition of pain to a state of mind makes it better, as in the case of the bad man who suffers.[17] It may thus be contended that in inflicting pain on such a man, we are bringing about an intrinsically better state of affairs. What are we to say about this? We must agree, I think, that the man who suffers because he realizes and repents his badness is in a better state of mind than one who gloats over it. But is it better that even bad men should suffer, regardless of why they suffer? Would Smith and Hickok have been better off, regardless of how they felt about their murders, if one of them could have developed cancer and the other had, by accident, broken his leg? This seems to me far from self-evident, and if so, then doubt is reflected back on the whole theory that guilt and suffering, as such, should go together.

Some Paradoxes of Retribution

That something is amiss with the theory is suggested, secondly, by the consideration that it would run counter to so much punishment which we now regard as justified. It would give us no ground for some punishments that we accept without question, and would lead us to the adoption of others which seem to be gravely wrong. Take an example of each. Retribution is supposed to be based on moral guilt. Very well—how, on that basis, are we to deal with treason? "Lord Haw-Haw" in the last war was a British subject who went over to the Nazis and worked for them actively to the end, when he was caught, tried, and hanged. Probably most of us would find it hard to develop much sympathy for him. Still, it does seem clear that a person might commit treason of this kind for morally high motives, turning against his country with sorrow, but with a conviction that she was bent on a course whose success would be tragic for the world. However mistaken he might be in such a view, he would not be acting immorally in the sense of going against what he thought to be right. Hence, no guilt of the kind required by the retributive theory would be involved in the case, and, so far, he should be set free. The retributionist may say he should still be imprisoned in the interest of public safety. But that is to go over to a different theory of punishment.

It may be asked, why not hold both theories at once, supplementing one by the other? But for such retributionists as Bradley and Kant, that is clearly impossible. If it is true, as Bradley insists, that a punishment given for any other reason than its being morally merited is "a gross immorality, a crying injustice, an abominable crime" then the imprisonment of the morally innocent traitor is itself an abominable crime. Here is a case in which the retributive theory can provide no ground for a punishment we feel to be called for. The theory would also insist, at times, on a punishment that seems uncalled for. We may take our example from the greatest of all retributionists, Kant:

> Juridical punishment can never be administered merely as a means for promoting another good, either with regard to the criminal himself or to civil society, but must in all cases be imposed only because the individual on whom it is inflicted *has committed a crime.* Even if a civil society were to dissolve itself by vote of all its members

(e.g. if a people, inhabiting an island, were to resolve to separate from one another and scatter themselves over the surface of the globe) nevertheless, before they go, the last murderer in prison must be executed. And this, that every man may receive what is the due of his deeds, and the guilt of blood may not rest upon a people which has failed to exact the penalty; for in that case, the people may be regarded as participators in the public violation of justice.[18]

This passage has been for two centuries a thorn in the retributionists' side. It exposes an element in their theory that looks painfully like sadism. "The guilt of blood" indeed! Kant is actually maintaining that this "guilt of blood" lies not with those who would kill the men in jail, but with those who would spare them. He would hold that even if there were no danger whatever to the societies in which these men would launch their lives anew, this chance should be denied them. Perhaps many retributionists would dissent from this view. But Kant's remorseless logic suggests where the theory tends to go if held in its purity. He may have been influenced here by his early pietistic Lutheranism, which never lost its emotional hold on him. It was part of this grim faith to believe that through the fault of remote ancestors men were sunk in infinite iniquity, that the Deity had accordingly imposed on them a penalty of infinite torture, and that, knowing this, they must still revere him as perfectly loving, wise and good.[1]

Retribution Conflicts with Forgiveness

The notion that pain should be imposed for guilt is neither self-evident, nor is it consistent with our convictions in crucial cases. Now for a third difficulty: It would make forgiveness wrong. Forgiveness does not mean, of course, that we first exact the penalty from a man, and then treat him as if he had never committed a crime at all. Nor (with all due respect to a great moralist) is it quite what Butler suggested. Butler thought that when someone did us an injury, we ". . . ought to be affected towards the injurious person in the same way as good men, uninterested in the case, would be, if they had the same just sense . . . of the fault, after which there will yet remain real good-will toward the offender."[19] This impersonality toward the offender is admirable; it dismisses the wound to *amour propre;* it renounces the resentment one is so likely to feel because it is oneself rather than someone else who has suffered offense. But surely the attitude here described is one of justice rather than forgiveness; it is quite consistent with exacting the full penalty imposed by custom or law. Forgiveness goes beyond this. It says: Even if by law or general consent I should be quite justified in exacting the penalty, I am not going to do it.

That forgiveness in this sense is a general duty is highly questionable; Paulsen thought Christianity irresponsible in stressing forgiveness to the neglect of seeing that justice was done.[20] It is clear, nevertheless, that forgiveness does often achieve what insistence on a penalty almost never achieves. That the person who has specially suffered, not some disinterested spectator, should put aside his resentment and refuse to return pain for pain is, as Rashdall says, ". . . an infinitely more convincing proof of love than punishment can ever be, and may, therefore, touch the heart as punishment will seldom touch it."[21] This, I take it, is one of the great discoveries of Christianity.

Such forgiveness the retributive theory would prohibit. The guilty man must be punished, and, as Kant said, if we remit the penalty, we are guilty ourselves. This seems to me an inhumanly doctrinaire rigorism. In the interest of what it conceives to be morality, it would impose a veto on morality at its highest. Nor will it do to say without further explanation that forgiveness should be admitted as an occasional exception to the general rule. If the exception is allowed for the greatest good, the suggestion is inevitable that the rule itself rests on the greatest good, which because of the unusual circumstances of this case must be reached in an unusual way.

Moral Guilt is Beyond Our Appraisal

To these three theoretical difficulties with retribution, we may add a final and practical difficulty. It is part of the retributive theory that the amount of penalty should correspond to the degree of guilt. But can we ever know or measure the degree of guilt? Precisely similar outward acts may spring from the most different states of mind. On a given night, three policemen are attacked in Los Angeles, and all are injured to the same extent. The first attack is made by a thief attempting to escape with his loot; the second by a Hollywood actor on a bibulous spree and prompted by a dare; the third by a Watts teenager who has been taught by family and playmates to regard policemen as public enemies. Suppose we were invited to appraise the amount of guilt involved in each of these outwardly similar cases—could we do it?

That we could not do it with any confidence is suggested by the wildly different penalties actually invoked in this country for the same crime, even when the authorities would not profess to be ascertaining anything so elusive as moral guilt.

> The time served for homicide in Texas is usually about 5½ years, in Illinois 16½ years. The maximum sentence for inducing abortion ranges from one year in Kansas to 20 years in Mississippi. For statutory rape, a man can get a $500 fine in Maine, 10 years in New York, 50 years in California, 99 years in New Mexico, and death in Delaware.[22]

Guilt attaches to the violation of what one knows or believes one ought to do. Who knows how clearly an offender does know or believe what he ought to do? Who knows the strength of his temptation to violate it? There are men so constituted and disciplined as to do their duty in a given situation as effortlessly as others would evade it. Oscar Wilde said of himself that he could resist anything except temptation, and for him, apparently, the exception became the rule. On the other hand, Professor Phelps of Yale remarked of his friend Dean Briggs of Harvard that ". . . the temptation to perform his duty was always strong, and if the duty were particularly disagreeable, the temptation became ungovernable.[23] Suppose one had to sit in judgment as to where on the scale of guilt and virtue to put Wilde and Briggs. One would get little help from their own verdict; Wilde would probably present himself with a verbal and moral carnation while Briggs was wringing his hands. No one can rightly judge his own guilt or guiltlessness; how can he hope to measure out pain upon the guilt of others?

We began by noting that the retributive theory sprang from instinctive resentment and revenge. We have granted resentment to be an indispensable check on wrongdoing. Such resentment tends almost irresistibly to pass over into revenge. Yet we have maintained that revenge, if it means the infliction of suffering simply for wrong done, is not morally defensible. It will certainly be a long time, if ever, before the public is convinced of this. What the theatre, the screen, and television would do without revenge is hard to imagine. Nevertheless it seems clear, on reflection, that revenge is the deliberate production of evil, evil that can neither undo what has been done, nor create some mystical atonement in which evil cancels evil. This does not mean, of course, that the infliction of suffering cannot be justified at all. It only means that punishment must be justified as every other act must in the end be justified, by its service to human welfare. We must build an inner dam that will keep anger and resentment from flooding destructively down the well-worn canyons of revenge. That these passions are too powerful and deadly to be unleashed except under the guidance of thought, has no doubt been known to all the saints. It has also been known to certain secular wise men. A tiny wisp of story has come floating down to us about Plato. A slave had misbehaved, and the philosopher had to deal with him. What did he do? All that the record gives us is one brief, tantalizing, pregnant remark: "I should have punished you if I had not been angry."

References

1. BRADLEY, F. H.: *Ethical Studies,* 2nd ed. Oxford, Clarendon Press, 1927, pp. 26-27.
2. Numbers 35:15.
3. *Ibid.,* 35:19.
4. JOSHUA 7:24.
5. HOBHOUSE, L. T.: *Morals in Evolution,* 5th ed. London, Chapman and Hall, 1925, p. 80.
6. RASHDALL, H.: *The Theory of Good and Evil,* 2nd ed. London, Oxford U. P. 1924, vol. 1., p. 291. The references to Maine and Stephen I also owe to Rashdall.
7. HAZLITT, W.: *The Plain Speaker.* London, Bell and Sons, 1907, p. 177.
8. LUCAS, F. L.: *Style.* London, Cassell and Co., 1955, p. 169. (Original in French).
9. *Ibid.,* pp. 135-36.
10. BRAILSFORD, H. N. (Ed): *Essays, Poems and Tales of Henry W. Nevinson.* London, Goilancz, 1948, pp. 253-54.
11. LECKY, W. E. H.: *The Rise and Influence of Rationalism in Europe,* 3rd ed. London, Longmans, Green and Co., 1866, vol. 2, p. 73.
12. SIDGWICK, H.: *Elements of Politics,* 2nd ed. London, Macmillan, 1897, p. 112.

13. McDougall, W.: *Social Psychology,* 12th ed. Boston, John W. Luce Co., 1917, p. 293.

14. Murray, G.: *The Crisis in Morals.* London, The Ethical Church, 1930, p. 29.

15. Hegel, G. W. F.: *Philosophy of Right,* T. M. Knox (Ed.). Oxford, Clarendon Press, 1942, sec. 100

16. McTaggart, J. M. E.: *Studies in Hegelian Cosmology,* 2nd ed. Cambridge U. P., 1918, p. 145.

17. Moore, G. E.: *Principia Ethica.* Cambridge U. P., 1903, p. 214.

18. Kant, I.: *Rechtslehre.* Secs. 331, 333.

19. Butler, J.: *Works,* W. E. Gladstone (Ed.). Oxford, Clarendon Press, 1897, vol. 2, sermon 9, sec. 13.

20. Paulsen, F.: *A System of Ethics,* trans. by F. Thilly. London, Kegan Paul, 1899, chap. 2, sec. 5.

21. Rashdall, *op. cit.,* vol. 1, p. 311.

22. *Time,* Dec. 31, 1965.

23. Phelps, W. L.: *Autobiography.* New York, Oxford U. P., 1939, p. 256.

SHOULD WE CONCEDE ANYTHING TO THE RETRIBUTIVISTS?

PETER H. HARE

I

I find myself in complete agreement with Professor Blanshard's masterly critique of the retributivist theory of punishment. However, he has included in his criticism what he calls, "Concessions to the Retributive Theory." Although I admire such generosity in a philosopher as eminent as Professor Blanshard, I feel strongly that this is not the place for concessions. I wish to argue that the utilitarian need make no concessions whatever to the retributivists, and further, that if such unnecessary concessions are made, serious consequences ensue. After considering, in turn, the five concessions made by Professor Blanshard, I shall end by pointing out that it is to the social scientists, not to the retributivists, that we should make concessions.

II

Professor Blanshard concedes to the retributivists that repulsion for causally inevitable moral evil is justified. "Cruelty," he says, "is . . . hateful and properly hated, even if causally inevitable." The utilitarian, however, is not without a justification for such repulsion. He points out how such moral feeling may be justified in terms of utility even in cases where the cruelty is inevitable. In the great majority of cases, cruelty is in some degree avoidable; if the psychological and social conditions force us to choose between no repulsion for cruelty at all, or repulsion for cruelty both avoidable and unavoidable, then it is better to choose the latter if it makes for greater good. The consistent utilitarian is not obliged to show that an isolated repulsion for cruelty (namely, one in which the cruelty is inevitable) makes for greater good. A *rule utilitarian,* as he is called, need show only that the rule of being repulsed by all cruelty has more utility than any alternative rule which is practically possible at present.

This does not show, as Professor Blanshard suggests, that repulsion for unavoidable cruelty is *in itself* justifiable. It shows only that under certain conditions it may be an evil but necessary means to the greater good.

This is not just a point of logic concerning the question of whether a pure and consistent utilitarianism is logically possible. Much more important is the fact that this concession has a strong tendency to encourage us to refuse to make a serious effort to decrease the number of cases in which it is a necessary evil to hate unavoidable cruelty. Instead we should proclaim the hating of unavoidable cruelty as *only* an evil but necessary means to greater good *in the present circumstances.*

It is conceded by Professor Blanshard that ". . . even the desire for revenge may be socially useful." Surely one can admit the social usefulness, under certain conditions, of the desire for revenge without making any concession to the retributivists. If one could somehow remove from the entire population the desire for revenge *without* instilling in everyone a commanding utilitarian interest in the greater good of all, obviously chaos would result. In that situation people would be left destitute of motivation to do anything in order to right wrongs. But the question is not whether *no* moral motivation is better than the vindictive one of the retributivists, but rather whether there are alternative motivations which would create greater good than desire for revenge. The utiliarian is not obliged to assert that desire for revenge is worse than no motivation at all. For the utilitarian to admit that under certain conditions the desire for revenge is at least temporarily necessary as a means to the greater good is not to make a concession in principle to the retributivist.

This second concession has the unfortunate consequence of tending to make people feel that under *any* conditions at least some desire for revenge is necessary to the greater good. This will make them much less apt to criticize constantly the connection between the desire for revenge and the greater good.

We must also, Professor Blanshard says, concede to the retributivist that we cannot merely hate the act and not the man. I am puzzled by the assumption that the utilitarian is obliged to be repulsed only by the act and not by the man. The utilitarian can consistently be repulsed by the man, in the sense that he recognizes that the individual's behavioral dispositions have an unfortunate effect on the greater good. These dispositions are just as genuine a threat to the greater good as any particular act. The utilitarian, however, hates the man only insofar as he has such dispositions. He rightly does not find everything else about the man guilty by association; he hates only what is causally relevant to future good; he is quite willing to admit that something more than isolated acts are causally relevant to the greater good.

This third concession has the unfortunate consequence of forcing individuals to either hate isolated acts or hate whole men. If they choose the former, their naiveté about the dispositions behind the acts makes it impossible to reform intelligently. If they choose the latter, they are indulging in a form of guilt by association which is hardly ideal.

Professor Blanshard wishes to concede that punishment can be partly justified as giving the individual the ability to " . . . *see himself as he is,"* and this insight, he suggests, has intrinsic value in addition to its possible contribution to future utilitarian results. But surely it is seriously misleading to describe this as a concession to the retributivists. Would it not be more accurately described as a concession to a *self-realization* theory of punishment? To justify punishment of someone in terms of its contribution to his self-knowledge is quite different from justification of the infliction of suffering on a man simply on the basis of his guilt. To miscall this a "concession" to retributivism is to invite unnecessarily all the ghastly consequences of retributivism.

In fact, what Professor Blanshard has done in this "concession" is to concede a weakness in utilitarianism as compared to a self-realization ethic. Yet, nowhere in his paper does he show us that such an ethic can provide a theory of punishment superior to that provided by utilitarianism. The utilitarian, of course, wishes to applaud the criticism of retributivism without conceding anything to the self-realizationist.

Finally, Professor Blanshard says that punishment has value as a contribution to the state *and the general good.* Like the fourth concession, this is, in reality, not a concession to retributivism but a concession to a self-realization ethic of the sort presented so eloquently by British absolute idealists at the beginning of the century. In this case, we have a concession which not only invites unnecessarily the dangers of retributivism but also appears to commit us to what may be an equally dangerous self-realization theory in which, in Bradley's famous imperative, we must " . . . be an infinite whole." Does Professor Blanshard wish, as it seems, to justify punishment as a contribution to the realization of the absolute self?

III

It is widely recognized that we must use the social sciences to find out which punishments, if any, are effective as reformatory and deterrent devices. That we must use the social sciences to determine when and in what forms the feeling of moral repulsion so dear to the retributivists is advantageous, is not so widely recognized. To make concessions to the retributivists is to discourage such investigation. The social scientists may find, after all, that, as a matter of empirical fact, such feelings are rarely, if ever, advantageous. Here, then, is a concession we must make to the social scientists. We must concede to them the right to decide by empirical test what the psychological and social consequences of moral feelings are.

Further, the social sciences must be used to discover how to increase systematically the most useful sorts of moral repulsion in the right places and at the right times. Professional philosophers reach an impasse here. They cannot hope to increase effectively the amount of the most useful feeling and to decrease the amount of the most damaging feeling by an appeal, however eloquent, to the development of a rational temper. Clearly, there are many otherwise "rational" men who are constantly taking the most vicious sort of revenge. Philosophy is impotent here, and there is no substitute for empirical investigation conducted by social scientists to discover precisely under what conditions men have the most useful moral feelings.

COMMENTARY ON PROFESSOR BLANSHARD'S CRITIQUE OF RETRIBUTIVE PUNISHMENT

Marvin K. Opler

Since I am in agreement with Professor Brand Blanshard's scholarly criticism of retribution, my comments can be only on the nature of the proofs. In saluting his product, but disputing his manner of reaching these conclusions, I must confess I am a social scientist, that is, an anthropologist and sociologist who has worked at times in the closely neighboring areas of social psychiatry and human values. I cannot agree that the root of crime lies *wholly* "in inward attitudes" and I put a very strong construction upon the adverb "wholly." It is pleasing that Professor Blanshard quickly adds that economic factors have relevance, but whereas he discusses their relevance only in our own society, it is necessary both to broaden and to extend this view to all societies in a very special evolutionary and dynamic sense.

The vast subcontinent of India has more poverty than we—and less crime. Primitive hunting and gathering peoples in totally marginal economies also show quite different and lower crime rates than we do.

Further, a colleague of mine in sociology, Dr. E. H. Powell, has published a paper entitled "Crime as a Function of Anomie."[1] Discussing Buffalo and several major cities in the United States, as well as European ones, he finds that in the turbulent aftermath of the Civil War and also in the period 1905-1917, a series of trends occurred including economic dislocations, institutional breakdowns, rapidly shifting values, and other forms of cultural upheaval. These were precisely the periods when crime thrived.

It is obvious a social scientist requires to know total rates of any phenomena which point to social disorganizational trends, and considers these when corrected against population numbers. He may, further, use other factors such as the per population rates of mental disorders, suicides, or delinquent behavior among youth so that these rates begin reflecting more than mere *individualized* phenomena of breakdown, to be seen, upon further analysis, as *group rates* which affect men and women differently, young and old, rich and poor, all in differing amounts. Concerning the larger relevance of the specific conditions in society affecting social classes, the sex groups, or age groupings, I know of no study which does not indicate that crime, or suicide, or psychiatric disorder (to cite only three instances of social pathology) are products of cultural conditions of existence.

The same variations are true of primitive or nonliterate societies. These too contain differential rates of crime, suicide, and mental disorder. Again, the primitive society which is breaking down rapidly because of colonial status or the heritage of conquest also has rising rates of crime, suicide, and psychiatric disorder, whereas those not subject to this negative form of rapid acculturation have better rates in all three categories than we do in the United States.[2]

Because of limits of space, a series of propositions are given as follows:

All societies and cultures have systems of sanctions. Radcliffe-Brown lists such possibilities as ritual, social, and legal (the latter he sometimes calls "retributive"). We hold that societies (not merely individuals) are sick or criminalistic. The societies with the poorest structure and functioning (such as Nazi Germany) have the most violent and frantic retributive systems exactly because of their social and cultural failure.

The above is no argument against legal reform, since law is a part, and a sensitive part, of the larger cultural framework.

Agreeing with the spirit, and I hope the intent, of Professor Blanshard's paper, we feel also, in social psychiatry, that *groups* as well as individuals require help in respect to conditions producing crime, suicide and poverty. In fact, the methods of social psychiatry and modern criminology are group rather than individually oriented. Yet, ultimately they help individuals in the group. The same would be true of legal reform as far as it goes.

Most important, the social scientist cannot abdicate the necessity of serious work, both quantitative and qualitative, in terms of human groups and human behavior in the plural. The yardsticks of human betterment may be quantified, as well as judged on individual, personalized levels. Professor Blanshard finally agrees; but I would hope, in place of his dichotomy of "they" (primitives and earlier societies) and "we" (in the U.S.A. presumably) one could apply cultural evolution to all peoples.

The hunting and gathering primitive societies which Professor Blanshard castigates as having retributive forms of punishment are really those in which such social sanctions as gossip, ridicule and ostracism are more prominent than retributive methods. Further, their notion of crime is markedly different. Such a thing as breaking incest regulations which we consider in the realm of social crimes, they would uniformly punish by death. Often they leave what we term "murder" up to the vendetta or revenge of an afflicted group. In the first case, their survival depends on optimum-sized social units which incest or breakages of their own curious rules of exogamy would seriously disrupt. Or, in Puerto Rico where young girls are shielded by their male relatives from sexual advances, there was *no* law against homicide, chiefly in the interests of protecting the avenging relatives who were expected to hunt down the culprit, which they often did in brutal ways sometimes resulting in death.

I am not advocating such a *status quo* in regard to the different techniques and targets of retribution. But we must note the utter irrationality in our own society which applies such sanctions as capital punishment or lifetime incarceration to murder no matter how psychiatrically ill the originator of the crime may be, but which at the same time refuses to expend proper sums for psychiatric science, or calls the erection of one or two housing projects by the euphemism of "slum clearance". One thinks also of the social problems beyond our border, when we vote billions for napalm bombing, for the helicopter surveillance of distant jungles, and for the widespread air strikes in the heavily populated terrain of South Vietnam. One wonders why one never hears of multibillion dollar programs in genuine slum clearance, or of crash programs on a large scale (larger certainly than Project Head-start) in the various fields of social and preventive psychiatry. Or there is even the curiously simple idea of arming the South Vietnamese village peasantry, rather than our erstwhile plan of putting them behind barbed wire enclosures in the so-called Strategic Village Program.

Criminology has been one of the areas in which social science has done little except to launch "demonstration programs" on a most limited basis, while at the same time it knows everything there is to know about the incidence of such things as crime, delinquency, suicide, and psychiatric disorder in the general population. The serious requirement is not to look backwards toward what is already known concerning individual causation, but to recognize that the tools for preventive criminology are ready and rusting from disuse. An important part of that recognition is the basic knowledge that crimes are social and cultural manifestations of widespread *group* problems, not simply of sick individuals, but of a sick society. Today we know what segments of this society require attention in terms of ethnic and subcultural groups, by class, sex, and age. Obviously, such knowledge is more valuable than the gross inflexibilities of retributive justice.

References

1. *Journal of Criminal Law, Criminology and Political Science*, 57:161-71, 1966.
2. OPLER, M. K.: *Culture, Psychiatry and Human Values.* Springfield, Thomas, 1956. Also, Opler, M.K.: *Culture and Social Psychiatry.* New York, Atherton, 1967.

   OPLER, M. K. (Ed.): *Culture and Mental Health.* New York, Macmillan, 1959. These references concern the low rates of psychologically-based disorders in unacculturated societies, especially of nonliterate cultures, when compared with our society. For an account of the high rates of psychiatric disorders in our own society, using New York City as an example, see Srole, L.; Langner, T.; Michael, S.; Opler, M.; and Rennie, T.A.C.: *Mental Health in the Metropolis: The Midtown Manhattan Study.* New York, McGraw, 1962.

CONCLUDING COMMENT

BRAND BLANSHARD

I am, of course, pleased to find that Dr. Hare and Dr. Opler are on my side of the fence regarding retribution, even though they think I managed to get over the fence myself only in ragged condition. I do not think my difference from either of my critics is very deep.

Dr. Hare thinks I conceded too much to the retributivists. He is inclined to draw a sharp line between the retributive and the utilitarian theory, and to find in any concession to the first, a criticism or abandonment of the second. My own line is less sharp; I think there are some features in which the theories may agree. Furthermore, he thinks some of my concessions to the retributivists are not really concessions to their theory at all. This is true. I used the term "concession" in a wider sense than his, perhaps misleadingly wide. At any rate I included among my concessions to them the recognition that they were guiltless of some of the more common charges against them. When this broader meaning of the term "concession" is cleared up, much of the difference between Dr. Hare and me is also cleared away. But not quite all. It may be well to look at his strictures in order.

I admitted I thought the retributionists right in regarding anger and repulsion as an appropriate attitude to take toward cruelty. Dr. Hare replies that this attitude can equally well be justified by the utilitarian standard. I agree. But the fact that it can be so justified is no reason against recognizing that the attitude is also intrinsically appropriate, as the retributionist holds. This appropriateness seems to me something that can be accepted by both theories.

I conceded to the retributionist, secondly, that the desire for revenge often serves a socially useful purpose. Dr. Hare replies: "Surely one can admit the social usefulness, under certain conditions, of the desire for revenge without making any concession to the retributivists." In a sense, this is clearly true; the only value we were granting to revenge was a purely utilitarian one. But my concern at this point was to defend the retributivist against an unjust and frequently repeated criticism. There have been many interpreters of Christian ethics who would say that in supporting revenge he was upholding a practice which was without justification of any kind. This seemed to me unfair to him, and I recalled that moralists as sensitive as Sidgwick and Gilbert Murray believed the sentiment of revenge to be at times legitimate and socially necessary. Revenge, therefore, was hardly to be set down as self-evidently and always evil.

Thirdly, I considered another line of attack on the retributivist. In his view, the most obvious ground for punishment is moral guilt, and guilt always lies in the man rather than in what he does; hence, he thinks we are justified in feeling an animus against the man himself. This has often been denied on the ground that our anger, hatred, or punishment should be directed not at the man, but at his action. This too seemed to me an implausible way of attacking the retributivist. For it is not practically or even theoretically possible to resent the action as distinct from the man; the action grows out of the motive, and the motive is part of the man. Dr. Hare points out that resentment directed against the whole man rather than against the evil side of him is unfair, and that resentment, rightly directed, is justifiable on utilitarian grounds. I agree on both points, but am not clear that such agreement is inconsistent with anything I have said.

Fourthly, I conceded some truth to Hegel's view that the prime aim of punishment is to awaken the agent to the wrong he has done, to make him see himself as he is. Dr. Hare points out that this is not strictly a retributive theory, since it does not advocate inflicting pain simply for guilt. Once more I agree; indeed I said this explicitly. Is my concession to Hegel then irrelevant? I do not think that for purposes of our discussion, it is. The name "retributory" has not been confined to any single theory, but has been historically given to a spectrum of theories distinguishable but closely related to each other through making punishment the requital of moral guilt. Hegel's theory is one of these, and an important one. It seemed to me that before selecting one of these views for intensive criticism (which I did) we should do well to take the theory in the broader sense and grant it everything we legitimately could. In this way we are more likely to do justice to the retributionists, whose thought is often emotional and inexact, than if we first define their theory narrowly and then proceed to demolish it.

I would make a similar comment on Dr. Hare's last criticism. The retributionists think we should punish moral guilt, and some people have thought this should be rejected on the ground that the state has no business at all with moral goodness or badness. This again seemed to me a wrong reason for rejecting retribution, since I think the main aim of the state is precisely to further the moral end, namely the greatest good of mankind. I believe the retributionists are right in saying that the state should act for moral ends, even though my way of determining what is moral differs greatly from theirs.

Dr. Hare scents danger at this point. In shooting my arrows at the retributionist, where am I standing myself? On good straightforward utilitarian ground, or on some dated and slightly camouflaged old theory like self-realization? Here I must confirm Dr. Hare's worst suspicions. I do not accept classical utilitarianism, and I do hold a view that is not far from that of the self-realizationists. I hold that the major maxim of ethics is: So act as to produce, if we can, the largest measure of self-realization among human beings generally, together with the happiness which normally attends it. If a defense of this is needed, as it obviously is, perhaps I may refer to my recent book on *Reason and Goodness,* where anyone interested will get as much of it as he wants, and rather more.[1]

It is fortifying to find that Dr. Opler, like Dr. Hare, would accept my conclusion about retribution. He differs from me chiefly in emphasis. The root of crime, I said, lies in the inward attitudes of individuals. The root of crime lies rather, he says, in a mal-organized, sick society. One can show this in conclusive fashion by connecting statistically the rising rates of rape, theft or assault with the economic factors of increasing poverty or crowded housing or unemployment. Such study will show us where and how to make our attack in the war on crime.

I hope there is no contradiction between this position and my own, for Dr. Opler is plainly right in insisting that what I should call *outward* factors like bad housing and low incomes do tend to produce crime. One can start with the fact from the last census, reported without emotional overtones, that 54 per cent of the people in the city of Washington are Negroes, and then take the report of the Chief of Police, reported with such overtones, that this part of the population is responsible for 85 per cent of the crimes. That fact is plainly important and calls for further statistical breakdown. This breakdown would no doubt show, as such analyses notoriously do, that the higher crime rate may be further cor-related with worse housing, worse pay, and worse unemployment. Such figures are undoubtedly helpful; they indicate things which must be done if the crime rate is to be reduced. Why, then, did I not show more enthusiasm about them?

First, because crimes are committed by individuals, and the most accurate of sociological generalizations never explains the individual. A man who belongs statistically where economic deprivation and crime reach their acme together may turn out to be embarrassingly saintly, and the ivy leaguer with every advantage may indulge in a rake's progress from prison to skid row. I dare say Charles Whitman fitted exactly into the statistician's pigeon-hole of those who would become pillars of society, up to the very morning he climbed that tower at Austin and picked off forty-four innocent persons below. We have been reminded by Douglas Bush that "Adolf Eichmann, examined by half a dozen psychiatrists, was pronounced, according to the best scientific standards, completely normal."[2] The individual is too complex to be explained by the kind of abstractions, however exhaustive, which social scientists can achieve.

There is a second reason for lack of emphasis on external conditions. It is that these conditions are only the remote, not the proximate or immediate causes of crime. Poverty and bad housing and the other economic factors do not issue in crime directly; they must act, if at all, through the medium of man's mind. Through minds having one set of beliefs, one set of hates and fears, one set of ambitions and moral standards, they will produce one kind of result; through another set, quite another. No cure for crime which does not take vigorous effect in the inner life will secure the hoped-for outward effect.

I stress this because, under the influence of physical science, we are coming to regard behavior as wholly a matter of physical responses, physically conditioned; there are eminent professors of psychology who are trying to abolish even the reference to an inner life. The explanation they give of human conduct, including criminal conduct, seems to me so remote from fact that if it were true, it would make no difference to anyone whether crimes were committed or not. If I may speak rather baldly again, a person with no statistics in his head, but with common sense, imagination and sympathy, will understand far better why a Negro youth resists a policeman, than will a man with a bale of statistics, but without access to another's mind. And the most effective antidote for the fear and resentment so prolific as an inner source of wrongdoing in the minority is a different inner attitude on the part of the majority. One example, perhaps Utopian, will suggest what I mean. A young friend of mine and his wife, with two charming children, wanted a third of their own, but in vain. They found a baby girl in a foundling home to whom they were particularly attracted, and they applied for her. She happened to be black, but they said that made no difference. The home hesitated in astonishment until it could be sure they meant what they said, and then gave them their wish. Whether, in view of all the conditions, they did the best for the child and themselves, I do not pretend to know. Of one thing I feel fairly sure: if this were the attitude of most Americans, the special worry of Washington's Chief of Police would be at an end.

References

1. BLANSHARD, B.: *Reason and Goodness*. New York, Humanities, 1961.
2. BUSH, D.: *Engaged and Disengaged*. Cambridge, Harvard U. P. 1966, pp. 224-25.

IV

THE CONTRIBUTION OF HEGEL, BECCARIA, HOLBACH AND LIVINGSTON TO GENERAL THEORY OF CRIMINAL RESPONSIBILITY

Mitchell Franklin

THE STUDY OF THEORY of criminal responsibility may begin with the confrontation between Beccaria and Hegel in section 100 of the latter's *Rechtsphilosophie.*

> The injury [the penalty] which falls on the criminal is not merely *implicity* just—as just, it is *eo ipso* his implicit will, an embodiment of his freedom; his right; on the contrary, it is also a right *established* within the criminal himself, i.e., in his objectively embodied wi'l, in his action. The reason for this is that his action is the action of a rational being and this implies that it is something universal and that by doing it the criminal has laid down a law which he has explicitly recognized in his action and under which in consequence he should be brought as under his right.

Hegel continues:

> As is well known Beccaria denied to the state the right of inflicting capital punishment. His reason was that it could not be presumed that the readiness of individuals to allow themselves to be executed was included in the social contract, and that in fact the contrary would have to be assumed. But the state is not a contract at all . . . nor is its fundamental essence the unconditional protection of the life and property of members of the public as individuals. On the contrary, it is that higher entity which even lays claim to this very life and property and demands its sacrifice. Further, what is involved in the action of the criminal is not only the concept of crime, the rational aspect present in crime as such whether the individual wills it or not, the aspect which the state has to vindicate, but also the abstract rationality of the individual's *volition.* Since that is so, punishment is regarded as containing the criminal's right and hence by being punished he is honoured as a rational being. He does not receive this due of honour unless the concept and measure of his

punishment are derived from his own act. Still less does he receive
it if he is treated either as a harmful animal who has to be made
harmless, or with a view to deterring and reforming him.[1]

Although Hegel thus opposes himself to Beccaria, nevertheless
they both agree, at least in part, that punishment for crime must be
based on the self-determination of the criminal. This unique starting point differentiates the theory of criminal law of both Hegel and
Beccaria from ordinary theory. Hegel knows this. "The theory of
punishment," he wrote, "is one of the topics which have [sic] come
off worst in the recent study of the positive science of law, because
in this theory the Understanding is insufficient; the essence of the
matter depends on the concept."[2]

Their theory that criminal responsibility is self-determined
means the criminal is a subject of law and not an object of law.
Beccaria said, "There is no liberty whenever the laws permit that,
in some circumstances, a man can cease to be a *person* and become
a *thing*. . . ."[3] D'Entrèves regards this as an anticipation of Kant,[4]
but it also seems to be an anticipation of Hegel, in that both
Beccaria and Hegel determine criminal responsibility by the will of
the accused. Hence, even the war criminals of World War II
were described as ". . . passive subjects of international law . . ."[5]
and not as objects thereof.

The question may now be asked, why the theory of self-determined responsibility of the criminal developed by both Beccaria
and Hegel nevertheless leads to directly opposed results with these
thinkers, both of whom were bourgeois and both of whom (one
an Italian and the other a German) were representatives of French
Encylopédisme.

The theory of self-determined criminal responsibility should be
understood as a development from the bourgeois alienation theory
of both Beccaria and Hegel. The concept of alienation is here used
with a juridical meaning. It signifies that human consciousness,
human labor and human language have been both volitionally
transferred, and seized or appropriated through socially created
means. Alienation, as here used, indicates that, although the social
subject, human life, has willingly passed into the social object, it has
been socially deprived of this object.[6] Indeed, because the social
subject has put his life into the object-artifact, the powerful object-

artifact itself has now become the subject. The genetic subject has veered and has become its own object. This conception of alienation (which, it must be repeated, is a conception of alienation as appropriation, as seizure, as domination, as *occupatio*) is opposed to the theory of alienation today held by existentialism. The latter is a theory of self-alienation of the subject from social life or even from the self. The latter is a theory, not of social appropriation, but of flight, of loneliness, of privacy, of distancing.[7] The latter theory may perhaps be noticed in the recent work of the Supreme Court of the United States, which is preoccupied with a theory of a constitutional right of privacy.[8] The two theories of alienation are opposed to each other because the existentialist theory of alienation does not admit that alienation originates in social seizure or social appropriation. From the point of view of an appropriative theory of alienation, existentialist alienation may be understood as secondary alienation in that the original social appropriation or seizure may result in the alienation of flight, of distancing, of privacy.[9]

The theory of self-determined criminal responsibility derives from the theory of appropriative alienation of the eighteenth century French Enlightenment. The Enlightenment, which culminated in the French and American bourgeois revolutions, set itself the double task, in part, of justifying inalienability (stated as inalienable rights of man) and, in part, of negating the existing acknowledged alienation. This is because the Enlightenment was directed against feudal alienation. As to such acknowledged feudal alienation, the ideology of the eighteenth century began with the thought that man was rational, but nevertheless existed in an irrational, or appropriated, or alienated, or feudal society. It was necessary, therefore, to alienate the alienation and thus to create rational or bourgeois social relations. Various theories explaining the alienation and justifying the negation or alienation of the alienation were developed. Among these was the theory of social contract. This conception seemed to explain the original alienation and also seemed to justify the retraction or dissolution or resolution of the original alienation, but only if the original alienation or social contract had been violated through the domination of irrational social relations or feudal law and custom. As Hegel points out, Beccaria's theory of criminal responsibility, at least in part, is founded on such social contract. Because the social contract had been willed, Hegel said, ". . . it could not be presumed that the readiness of individuals to allow themselves to be executed was included . . . [by the subject of law] . . . in the social contract and that in fact the contrary would have to be assumed."[10] What may now be said is that the Enlightenment, beginning with the feudal alienation of human reason, understood the problem of negating the alienation as a problem of education through enlightened or bourgeois law. In his *Supplement to Bougainville's Voyage,* Diderot said, "If the laws are good, morals are good; if the laws are bad, morals are bad. . . ."[11] If so, as Holbach indicated, criminality can be seen as the consequence of feudal consciousness caused by feudal social relations or feudal circumstances. Rational education would end the feudal circumstances which had caused the crime. The task of criminal law thus was not to destroy the criminal but to overcome the criminal circumstances. This is the real meaning of Beccaria's social contract theory of criminal punishment.

Perhaps it may be suggested that historically the theory of social contract is not entirely invalid. As Roman law began in kin-organized society, it is older than the Roman state. In this society, competence to make determinations was founded on self-determination. The process began with an undertaking to submit the dispute to an arbitral process. This procedural contract or *litis contestatio* may have been a source for social contract theory of the state. Furthermore, during the emergence of the Roman state *litis contestatio* remained valid because it became an aspect of the power of *intercessio* by which a plebeian tribune could, if desirable, refuse to concur in patrician determinations affecting plebeians.

Adhémar Esmein says Beccaria's slender volume ". . . was a petition which Europe used to present to its sovereigns."[12] In general, his thought passed also to the United States at an early date through Thomas Jefferson[13] and John Adams.[14] Both Jefferson and Adams studied the Italian text of Beccaria.

Although it has not been acknowledged by the Supreme Court of the United States, aspects of Beccaria's thought relative to infamy appear in the vital Fifth Amendment, which I therefore have called the *lex* Beccaria. In a dissenting opinion, Justice Douglas at one time recognized Beccaria's relationship to this text.[15] The course of the reception may be said to proceed from Beccaria to John Adams, into the constitution of Massachusetts and thence into the Fifth Amendment. However, the influence of Beccaria was most powerfully developed in the United States at a later date through the theory of criminal law and *projets* of the codes of Edward Livingston. Livingston not only condemned the death penalty, but explained crime as a consequence of poverty and unemployment. Early in the nineteenth century he proposed state action to relieve unemployment and thus to end criminality. His thinking may be related to that of Diderot and Holbach. The latter believed it was not the criminal but the feudal state which was guilty of the crime. This theory will be discussed later.

As has been indicated, Hegel's theory of criminal law, like Beccaria's, is a theory of self-determined punishment. Like Beccaria, Hegel holds that the criminal is a *subject* of and not an *object* of law, because the criminal puts his will into his own punishment. Although Hegel approves of the diminished resort to death as a punishment,[16] his theory is more drastic than Beccaria's in that Hegel says all punishment inflicted on the wrongdoer is self-determined, whereas Beccaria believes the criminal wills the acceptance of certain punishments, but not the penalty of death. It was the will of Beccaria's criminal only to overcome or to negate feudal criminal law and procedure in order to introduce certain bourgeois theory of criminal law. However, it was the will of Hegel's criminal to be punished in accordance with the requirements of the totality of bourgeois legal institutions *in vigor* in the positive state. Beccaria's criminal directs his will to defeating feudal criminal law before the French Revolution. Hegel's criminal directs his will to maintaining the criminal law of bourgeois France after the French Revolution, and also to justifying the criminal law in a Germany which was still feudal and not yet bourgeois. Beccaria's theory of criminal law is the theory of criminal law of the bourgeoisie seeking to conquer and to destroy the feudal state. Hegel's theory of criminal law is essentially that of the bourgeoisie after this class has conquered the feudal French state, or believes that the preconditions for such conquest have been created in Germany because of certain political reform there.

In considering the thought of Hegel, it is always important to determine, if possible, whether he is acting as representative of the French bourgeoisie, who had won plenary state power, or whether he is responding to the needs of the weak German bourgeoisie, who in his time had not yet created a bourgeois Germany. Although Hegel's *Rechtsphilosophie* may waver between these two concerns, it may be suggested that Hegel's theory of criminal law is essentially that of the successful French bourgeoisie. This may be said for three reasons:

First, Hegel's theory of contract is a bourgeois will theory, rejecting unsuitable elements of the Roman law theory of contract. Moreover, his theory of property is essentially bourgeois, based on the Romanist idea of ownership established by the French civil code. It may be said that his defense of bourgeois property ideas against feudal property ideas is extraordinarily brilliant. He rejects the ideas of divided property which obtained under feudalism, replacing them with the French idea of uncontradicted ownership. This appears in his discussion of the European feudal division of property into *dominium directum* and *dominium utile*.[17] This was a distinction between strict law ownership and equitable ownership, the latter of which was the negation of the first. Because Hegel condemned the feudal division between legal and equitable ownership, he separates himself from the contradictory feudal property ideas of Anglo-American law, which even now consecrates the feudal contradiction between common-law property and the opposed property conceptions of the Anglo-American chancery or Anglo-American equity. It is true that Hegel also justified German feudal law of primogeniture, which served no bourgeois interest at the time of the French Revolution. However, Hegel justifies feudal primogeniture quite late in the *Rechtsphilosophie* and hence relates it not to his theory of bourgeois property, but to his defense of his German monarchical regime, with which the *Rechtsphilosophie* concludes. This was Hegel's contradiction, which the young Marx éxploited.[18]

Second, *what is most important to state here is that Hegel establishes the mission of criminal law to be that of protecting and securing the above mentioned bourgeois property rights.* His theory of self-determined criminality is a theory which

Hegel immediately relates to his considerations affecting bourgeois contract and bourgeois property. As Hegel discusses bourgeois contract, bourgeois property, and crime in their dialectical relations, it may be suggested he is also presenting a theory of bourgeois crime.

Third, *in general, Hegel, by beginning the Rechtsphilosophie with abstract law,* is following certain bourgeois legal theory of the Enlightenment, such as Diderot's (already quoted) that law is prior to and explains morality, so that good laws explain good morals and bad laws explain bad morals. The mechanistic Enlightenment justified the priority of abstract bourgeois law as the activity of an unhistorical prince who promulgates rational laws in order to overcome the irrational morality or irrational customs of feudalism. Hegel, as a dialectical idealist, explains the priority of abstract law, not as the activity of an unhistoric, bourgeois prince, but as the self-activity of the bourgeois form of law, perhaps as the self-motion of Kantian formalism.

Hegel's starting point, in which abstract law precedes morality, not only reflects the *Encyclopédiste* activist theory of the hegemony of bourgeois law over feudal morality, but also directly confronts the feudal *Volksgeist* theory of the powerful German historical school of law, headed by Savigny, who was Hegel's colleague at Berlin and who was one of the mightiest forces in twenty-five centuries of Roman law. Savigny (whose thinking is related to the objective idealism of Hegel's opponent, Schelling) fought the reception within Germany of bourgeois legal theory of the French Enlightenment. Savigny explained law as the revelation of the idealistic *Volksgeist* or national spirit, manifested through popular custom. As Germany was then feudal, Savigny's theory of law justified feudalism and aristocratism. The ideological hostility between Hegel and Savigny explains why Hegel supported codification of law and why Savigny opposed it. Because he begins the *Rechtsphilosophie* with abstract law, Hegel could overcome Savigny's feudal or acquired-rights legal conceptions by means of certain bourgeois *Encyclopédiste* educational-legal ideas, thus negating Savigny's feudal alienation. Therefore, Hegel does not justify the *Rechtsphilosophie* as such with the superstructural theory of law advanced by Montesquieu in *Esprit des lois,* even though he recognized Montesquieu as a very important precursor. In Section 3 of the *Rechtsphilosophie* Hegel says:

> . . . Montesquieu proclaimed the true historical view, the genuinely philosophical position, namely that legislation both in general and in its particular provisions is to be treated not as something isolated and abstract but rather as a subordinate moment in a whole, interconnected with all the other features which make up the character of a nation and an epoch. It is in being so connected that the various laws acquire their true meaning and therewith their justification.

Having said in Section 90 of the *Rechtsphilosophie* that "In owning property I place my will in an external thing, and this implies that my will, just by being thus reflected in the object, may be seized in it and brought under compulsion,"[19] Hegel, in Section 94, says that bourgeois, or formal or "Abstract right [law] is a right [law] to coerce, because the wrong which transgresses it is an exercise of force against the existence of my freedom in an external thing."[20] In Section 99, that is, in the section immediately preceding his discussion of Beccaria's attack on capital punishment, Hegel conceives that criminal punishment is the negation by coercion of the negation by coercion of the subjective right of the victim of the crime. He wrote: "Hence to injure [or penalize] this particular will as a will determinately existent, is to annul the crime, which otherwise would have been held valid, and to restore the right."[21]

As has been said, the bond between Beccaria and Hegel is that each conceives of the bourgeois criminal as a subject of law and not as an object of law, although Hegel of course does not agree with Beccaria that the theory of social contract justifies the concurrence between them. As has been said, Kant also held that the criminal was a subject of law,[22] and is criticized therefore by Holmes in *The Common Law:*

> It is objected that the preventive theory is immoral, because it overlooks the ill-desert of wrongdoing, and furnishes no measure of the amount of punishment, except the lawgiver's subjective opinion in regard to the sufficiency of the amount of preventive suffering. In the language of Kant, it treats man as a thing, not as a person; as a means, not as an end in himself. It is said to conflict with the sense of justice, and to violate the fundamental principle of all free

communities, that the members of such communities have equal rights to life, liberty, and personal security. In spite of all this, probably most English-speaking lawyers would accept the preventive theory without hesitation. As to the violation of equal rights which is charged, it may be rep'ied that the dogma of equality makes an equation between individuals only, not between an individual and the community. No society has ever admitted that it could not sacrifice individual welfare to its own existence. If conscripts are necessary for its army, it seizes them, and marches them, with bayonets in their rear to death. It runs highways and railroads through old family places in spite of the owner's protest, paying in this instance the market value, to be sure, because no civilized government sacrifices the citizen more than it can help, but still sacrificing his will and his welfare to that of the rest.[23]

The authors of *Geschichte der Philosophie* write: "Under the historical conditions in Germany at the beginning of the nineteenth century the Hegelian philosophy of law had a progressive social connotation, in so far as it opposed bourgeois law to feudal arbitrariness."[24] Piontkowski in *Hegelslehre über Staat und Recht und seine Strafrechtstheorie* wrote that Hegel ". . . saw in the criminal not only the object of punishment, but a subject of law. . . ."[25] Piontkowski showed that Marx in the *New York Tribune* related Hegel's conception that the abstract criminal was a subject of law to Kant's conception, and also related the theory of both of these German thinkers to similar ideas of Heine.[26]

However, because of his historical position, Hegel could not realize the legal goal he sought. As has been said, he was a theorist for the victorious bourgeois French Enlightenment. He was also a theorist of the weak bourgeoisie in a Germany which was then still feudal. But it was not possible in any bourgeois society for the criminal to will his own punishment because all bourgeois society rests on an unbridgeable scission, as Holmes suggested, between general will and particular or private or arbitrary will. Hence Marx and Engels said:

Hegel holds that the criminal must as a punishment pass sentence on himself. *Gans* developed this theory at greater length. In Hegel this is a *speculative disguise* of the old *jus talionis* that Kant developed as the *only legal penal theory*. Hegel makes self-judgment of the criminal no more than an '*Idea*,' a mere speculative interpretation of the *current empiric penal code*. He thus leaves the mode of application to the respective stages of development of the state, i.e., he leaves punishments as it is . . . A *penal* theory that at the same time sees in the criminal the *man* can do so only in *abstraction,* in imagination, precisely because *punishment, coercion,* is contrary to *human* conduct. Besides, this would be impossible to carry out. Pure subjective arbitrariness would take the place of the abstract law because it would always depend on official "honest and decent" men to adapt the penalty to the individuality of the criminal. Plato admitted that the *law* must be one-sided and must *make abstraction* of the individual. On the other hand, under *human* conditions punishment will *really* be nothing but the sentence passed by the culprit on himself. There will be no attempt to persuade him that *violence* from *without,* exerted on him by others, is violence exerted on himself by himself. On the contrary, he will see in *other* men his natural saviours from the sentence which he has pronounced on himself; in other words the relation will be reversed.[27]

In his own theory of self-determined criminality, Hegel seized the particular or private will of the subject of law and attributed to him by mediation or negation[28] the general will of objective idealism to be punished for his particular act. Hegel negated (punished) the attempted negation of the subjective right of the victim of the criminal (the crime) within and through the mediated or negated will of the criminal himself. But because of his situation in the bourgeois world, Hegel's solution was a solution founded in an appropriative alienation, or seizure or *occupatio* of the will of the accused. Hence, appropriative alienation by the state of the willed act and of the consciousness of the accused explains both Beccaria's eighteenth century social contract theory and Hegel's nineteenth century objective idealist theory of mediated criminal responsibility.

As has been indicated, Hegel states his theory of criminal law in his treatment of abstract law, prior to his more concrete categories of *Moralität, Sittlichkeit,* family, civil society and the state, which he unfolds only subsequently to abstract law. Hegel thus begins with a criminal who already is an abstracted or alienated person. He need not fully consider whether the particular criminal will of the abstract criminal law is not already a general will because such a particular will enters the world and exists in the world as the complex of the social relations which each individual is.[29] Hegel abstracts or alienates this social, particular individual, so that he begins with an egoistic or bourgeois, individualistic particular will to which a general or an Hellenic will may then be attributed. Hegel does this because bourgeois social relations were not Hellenic. In his remark in Section 190 of the *Rechtsphilosophie,* Hegel says:

> In [abstract] right [law], what we had before us was the person; in the sphere of morality, the subject; in the family, the family-member; in civil society as a whole, the burgher or *bourgeois.* Here at the standpoint of needs . . . what we have before us is the composite idea which we call *man.* Thus this is the first time, and indeed properly the only time, to speak of *man* in this sense.[30]

Thus, Hegel's abstract criminal begins as an historically partitioned or virtually quality-less or relation-less criminal. In the realm of abstract law, he is nothing more than this. Hegel excludes from this realm the idea that his criminal man is a man if and only if he is recognized as an historic complex or "composite" of all his social relations. This is why Hegel's criminal enters as an abstracted or as an alienated subject of abstract criminal law. In the twentieth century a remote kinsman of Hegel's abstract man will appear as the radically unhistoric, entirely empty *pour soi* of Sartre. The *pour soi* is that which begins without any historic relations. Hegel's abstract criminal, restated as a Sartrean *pour soi,* thus in truth reappears as Kantian *an sich,* as a thing-in-itself, or as a thing without social relations. But such a Kantian thing-in-itself, as Hegel showed elsewhere than in the *Rechtsphilosophie,* is a nothing because it has no social relations.[31] Kant's *en soi,* or thing-in-itself, is the precursor of Sartre's *pour soi* (though the other abstract parent derives from Sartre's revolt from Husserl's theory of knowledge). Such a *pour soi,* or nothing, indeed may will its own punishment. But such punishment will not fall on a nothing, but on real historic man, on the man who also is Sartre's proletarian waiter, on man who is a man because he is a complex of historic social relations.

Therefore, Hegel's theory of criminality, as drastically radicalized by Sartre, would be a theory of appropriative alienation, even though such abstract criminal or empty *pour soi* may be, as has been said earlier in this paper, a subject of abstract criminal law and not its object. This criticism of Sartre does not mean he does

not surpass and overcome rival phenomenologists and existentialists. But, unlike Sartre, Hegel's own criminal is not totally unhistorical, though he is an abstract criminal. The French Revolution
had made him at least a citizen or subject of law. Hegel himself
limits the abstraction or alienation of the criminal. He considers
criminality and the punishment of criminality as a relation (though
it is a relation through alienation) of an abstract, particular will
to a general will. This relation is sufficient for Hegel. Such Hegelian
abstract or alienated subject of the abstract criminal law has been
created in order to create responsibility for the violation of bourgeois property and other rights grounded therein. Writing of Hegel's
Jugendschriften, Peperzak asks:

> The law violated is transformed into its *contrary* in order to con-
> demn the criminal as the latter has condemned his victim. The
> situation which results from the infraction is summed up therefore
> in the opposition of an *universal* law (having the *content* of the
> crime) and of the ineradicable act, which as to its *form,* is *particular.*
> From that time, the anguishing question emerges: how is this recon-
> ciled with this just law?[32]

What Peperzak here requires is that Hegel establish the connection
between particular will and the general will.

> Having maintained against Beccaria that the externalized will of
> the criminal is both a particular and an 'universal' will, and that it
> is the attributed or constructive 'universal' will to punish crime, the
> 'universal' will of the criminal wills and justifies his own punishment,
> [the present writer has said]. Thus, for Hegel the will of the criminal
> externalized in the criminal act is self-directed against the criminal.
> The will of the criminal seems to have become a *res* or a thing or
> an object, which has won its independence from the criminal, al-
> though it has been brought into the world by the criminal. It seems
> to have turned against him and to dominate him. Here the external-
> ized particular will of the criminal is appropriated or alienated as
> an Hegelian 'universal' which wills and justifies the punshment. What
> had been criminal will-for-self, realized in the world, becomes a
> repressive will-against-self, that is will-for-other, will-for-the-state.[33]

In Section 104 of the *Reschtsphilosophie,* Hegel says of the will
of the criminal subject of law: "Its personality — and in abstract
right [law] the will is personality and no more — it now has for
its object. . . ." However, Hegel does not here declare that in ab-

stract law will-for-self has thus become will-for-other, will-for-the-state. The will, he says: ". . . is a free will not only in itself but for itself also. . . ."[34] In the addition to Section 104, he writes of the will:

> It must in its own eyes be subjectivity, and have itself as its own object. This relation to itself is the moment of affirmation, but it can attain it only by superseding its immediacy. The immediacy superseded in crime leads, then, through punishment, i.e., through the nullity of this nullity, to affirmation, i.e. to morality.[35]

In the *Phänomenologie* Hegel discusses the connection between the particular will and the general will and shows in mystical fashion how the social will (rather the will of the bourgeois state) appropriates, dominates, or devours the particular will. In considering the individual in "the law of the heart," Hegel says:

> . . . it finds that reality animated by the consciousness of all, and a law for all hearts. It learns through experience that the reality in question is an ordinance infused and endowed with life, and learns this, indeed, by the fact that it actualizes the law of its own heart. For this means nothing else than that individuality becomes its own object in the form of universality, without however recognizing itself therein.[36]

In order to complete such thought it may be said that social life or the state seizes the abstract individual will and directs his individuality against his individuality. Hyppolite writes that here ". . . I perceive myself as a stranger to myself, engaged in a sequence of operations which are at once mine and not mine. I am *alienated* from myself."[37]

This conception of alienation not only explains Hegel's theory of the self-determined will of the criminal but explains Hegel's social theory in general. He wrote in the *Phänomenologie*:

> Language and labour are outer expressions in which the individual no longer retains possession of himself *per se,* but lets the inner get right outside him, and surrenders it to something else . . . into an other, and thereby puts itself at the mercy of the element of change, which transforms the spoken word and the accomplished act, and makes something else out of them than they are in and for themselves as actions of a particular determinate individual.[38]

Hegel's theory of criminal law is therefore a theory of bourgeois social science in general, in that he makes alienation permanent in human history and does not differentiate human *praxis* from such alienation.[39] But in the *Ökonomisch-philosophische Manuskripte* of 1844, Marx wrote of alienation that:

> Religion, family, state, law, morality, science, art, etc. are only *particular* modes of production, and fall under its general law. The positive transcendence of *private property* as the appropriation of human life, is, therefore, the positive transcendence of all estrangement. . . .[40]

The antecedents for Hegel's theory of the self-determined guilt of the criminal may be sensed in Hegel's *Jugendschriften,* as Peperzak suggests, although his discussions in the latter seem to emphasize immediacy rather than mediation or negation or connection. In *Der Geist des Christentums und sein Schicksal* (the text of which is said to have been written before 1800)[41] Hegel states thoughts[42] which may be related to his theory of criminal responsibility, as stated in the *Rechtsphilosophie,* which was published in 1821. Mario Rossi, in *Marx e la dialettica hegeliana,* (1960) also agrees that the two writings should be considered together in order to understand Hegel's theory of criminal responsibility.[43] What may be discovered in *Der Geist des Christentums und sein Schicksal* is, as Lukács says,[44] more, therefore, than theology and more than the ethics of Kant. Although Hegel seems immersed in religion and theology, underneath the surface he is exploring the dialectic of social responsibility.

What Hegel offers in *Der Geist des Christentums und sein Schicksal* is a theory of human responsibility in the social world and to the law. He seems to be groping toward a theory of human responsibility which is self-determined, but which is also other-determined. Such a theory of responsibility requires appropriative alienation in bourgeois societies founded on private property. Indeed, in *Der Geist des Christentums und sein Schicksal,* Hegel is conscious that he is in the world of private property.

> The fate of private property has become too powerful for us to tolerate reflections on it, to find its abolition thinkable. But this at least is to be noticed, that the possession of riches, with all the rights as well as the cares connected with it, brings into human life definitive details whose restrictedness prescribes limits to the virtues. . . .[45]

Perhaps Hegel is here reflecting the pessimism of the abbé de Mably, the French utopian communist. It is not possible to say that Hegel knew the work of Mably, though in 1825 Hegel wrote that Mably's history of France was "indispensible."[46]

In *Der Geist des Christentums und sein Schicksal,* Hegel says:

Punishment is the effect of a transgressed law from which the trespasser has torn himself free but on which he still depends; he cannot escape from the law or from punishment or from what he has done. Since the characteristic of the law is universality, the trespasser has smashed the matter of the law, but its form—universality—remains. The law, whose master he believed he had become, remains . . . but in its content it now appears in opposition to him because it has the shape of the deed which contradicts what previously was the law, while the content of the deed now has the shape of universality and is law. This perversion of the law, the fact that it becomes the contrary of what it was before, is punishment. Because the man has cut himself loose from the law, he still remains in subjection to it. And the law, as a universal, remains, so too does the deed, since it is particular.[47]

Hegel distinguishes criminal responsibility from destiny. He says:

Only the trespasser is not reconciled with the law, whether (a) the law is in his eyes something alien, or whether (b) it is present in him subjectively as a bad conscience. (a) The alien power which the trespasser has created and armed against himself, this hostile being, ceases to work on him once it has punished him. . . . (b) In the bad conscience (the consciousness of a bad action, of one's self as a bad man) punishment, once suffered, alters nothing. For the trespasser always sees himself as a trespasser. . . .[48]

Later Hegel writes:

When the trespasser feels the disruption of his own life (suffers punishment) or knows himself (in his bad conscience) as disrupted, then the working of his fate commences, and this feeling of a life disrupted must become a longing for what has been lost. The deficiency is recognized as a part of himself, as to what was to have been in him and is not. This lack is not a not-being but is life known and felt as not being. To have felt this fate is to fear it; and this is a feeling quite different from the fear of punishment. The former is a fear of a separation, an awe of *one's self;* fear of punishment is fear of something alien, still in the fear of punishment the punishment is something alien unless the fear is conceived as fear of being unworthy. In punishment, however, there is added to the feeling of unworthiness the reality of a misfortune, i.e., the loss of well-being which one's concept [or essence] has lost and which therefore one no longer deserves. Hence punishment presupposes an alien being who is lord of this reality [i.e., who inflicts the pain of punishment], and fear of punishment of him. In fate, on the other had, the hostile power is the power of life made hostile; hence fear of fate is not the fear of an *alien* being.[49]

Here Hegel's alienation takes somewhat the form of reification. The alienation is not perceived as appropriation by the other because it is masked or misunderstood, so that the appropriated or alienated person regards himself as his own enemy; his own will as a subject dominating him as its object; his own labor as his own master; his own life as his own death, and, in criminal law, his own act declaring his own punishment, and so on. But in his own *Jugendschriften,* Marx, who probably never encountered Hegel's *Jugendschriften,* perceived that reification was an aspect of appropriative alienation:

Not the gods, not nature, but only man himself can be this alien power over man [Marx wrote in the *Ökonomisch-philosophische Manuskripte* in his considerations concerning the moment of appropriation or occupation in alienation.] We must bear in mind the above-stated proposition that man's relation to himself only becomes *objective* and *real* for him through his relation to the other man. Thus, if the product of his labour, his labour *objectified* is for him an *alien,* hostile, powerful object independent of him, then his position towards it is such that someone else is master of this object, someone who is alien, hostile, powerful, and independent of him. If his own activity is to him an unfree activity, then he is treating it as activity performed in the service, under the dominion, the coercion and the yoke of another man. . . .[50]

Through his ideas of reification, through his ideas in which the subject makes himself his own object by the reification of his crime, Hegel lay down the philosophical foundation for a body of great literature. He writes:

. . . only through the killing of life, is something alien produced. Destruction of life is not the nullification of life but its diremption, and the destruction consists in its transformation into an enemy. It is immortal, and, if slain, it appears as its terrifying ghost

which vindicates every branch of life and lets loose its Eumenides.
The illusion of trespass, its belief that it destroys the other's life
and thinks itself enlarged thereby, is dissipated by the fact that the
disembodied spirit of the injured life comes on the scene against
trespass, just as Banquo who came as a friend to Macbeth was not
blotted out when he was murdered but immediately thereafter
took his seat, not as a guest at the feast, but as an evil spirit. The
trespasser intended to have to do with another's life, but he has
only destroyed his own. . . . In his arrogance he has destroyed
indeed, but only the friendliness of life; he has perverted life into
an enemy. It is the deed indeed which has created a law whose
domination now comes on the scene; this law . . . is the unification,
in the   concept, of the equality between the injured, apparently
alien life, and the trespasser's own forfeited life. It is now for the
first time that the injured life appears as a hostile power against
the trespasser and maltreats him as he has maltreated the other.
Hence punishment as fate is the equal reaction of the trespasser's own
deed, of a power which he himself has armed, of an enemy made
an enemy by himself.[51]

Mario Rossi perceives here the meaning of certain literature
"from Hugo to Dostoevski."[52]

Hegel's theory that the criminal wills his own punishment is
founded on appropriative alienation or on reification, because
contemporary social relations are founded on appropriative alienation. Without such appropriation or reification Hegel cannot
make the transition from the egoism of private interest and private
will to social interest and social will. Here Hegel's mediations
or negations cannot be justified. Hegel's effort to Hellenize, as
it were, the private property ideas of the bourgeois world merely
legitimates the social domination of private property. Hegel was
not unmindful of his problem. He realized why the eighteenth
century Enlightenment before him had also failed in its effort
to solve the antagonism between particular and general interest.
In the *Phänomenologie* he considers the dialectic of "pleasure"
or of freedom and necessity. "Pleasure" or the utilitarian theory
of the eighteenth century seemed dialectically to require necessity;
and "virtue" confronted "the course of the world." Contrary
to Jefferson, Hegel shows that this eighteenth century idea of
virtue failed because of "the course of the world."[53] This deserves more than passing notice because of its impact on the

Constitution of the United States, which requires that the United States guarantee republican form of government in the particular states. This consecrates Montesquieu's theory of republican virtue. Republican virtue, Montesquieu said, ". . . may be defined as love of the laws and of our country. As such love requires a constant preference of public to private interest, it is the source of all private virtues. . . . This love is peculiar to democracies."[54]

Hegel, who regarded Montesquieu as a precursor, understood what Montesquieu was attempting and why Montesquieu had failed. More specifically, Hegel's effort through appropriative alienation and reification to relate the particular will of the criminal to the universal will of punishment must be understood as an aspect of Hegel's effort to solve the crisis of bourgeois social relations. Hegel's effort may be called the Hellenization of the bourgeois world[55] on a higher level than that of antiquity. It was Hegel's conception that the Athenian world, as it emerges from kin-organized society into the world of private property, had broken the unity of social life. As general and particular life were thus split asunder, the historical mission of mankind was to negate the negation, or to alienate the alienation, or to restore the unity on a more concrete and on a higher level. Hegel's love of Greek tragedy in part was caused by its content, which considered the crisis in its immediacy. For Hegel, human history, in general, becomes the history of historic freedom. Such history is social negation of an historic appropriative negation, achieved in and through the historic appropriative alienation itself. As alienation of the alienation is freedom realized through and within the alienation, the alienation may be understood as the historic necessity, and historic freedom as the negation of such historic necessity. Through their motions human work, labor, language, and *praxis* generate both the appropriative alienation and its negation.

Thus, although Hegel's attempt at a theory of criminal law fails because it justifies *occupatio* and reification of the will of the abstract criminal, there emerges from this failure a triumph of social theory, perhaps one of the most important intellectual accomplishments of the nineteenth century. It is the conception of the alienation of the alienation. This is a theory of the unity-in-opposition of historical necessity and historical freedom, in which historical freedom both requires and negates already historically posited necessity.[56]

However, contemporary bourgeois social and legal theory, including criminal law, has not accepted this theory of the unity of necessity and freedom. Present-day social theory wavers between theory of absolute necessity and theory of absolute freedom of will. The question which is usually asked in bourgeois criminal law is whether the accused had the arbitrary, or abstract, or formal freedom or "intention" required for conviction for the particular crime.

A reading of Hegel's *Jugendschriften* indicates Hegel was there exploring the relations of freedom and necessity. Perhaps he felt this problem chiefly in his considerations of destiny rather than in his discussion of criminal laws. Putting it in his own way, Hyppolite says:

> . . . the question which is posed is rightly that of the relations of reason and liberty as that of the irrational and the rational. . . . If we no longer consider this problem under its theoretical aspect, but under its practical aspect we discover still another opposition included in it . . . that of *constraint* and of *liberty*.[57]

In Section 104 of the *Rechtsphilosophie,* where he is considering criminal law and discussing the transition from abstract law to morality, Hegel says, ". . . the right [law], upheld in the face of the explicitly independent single will, is and is recognized as an actual on the score of its necessity."[58] What Hegel had discussed in Section 100 as the problem of establishing the unity of the universal or general will and the particular will of the criminal, in Section 104 is dialectically related to the problem of establishing the relation of necessity and freedom. And in the *Enzyklopädie,* he wrote:

> This truth of necessity, therefore, is *Freedom.* . . . Necessity is often called hard, and rightly so, if we keep only to necessity as such, *i.e.,* to its immediate shape. Here we have, first of all, some state or, generally speaking, fact, possessing an independent subsistence; and necessity primarily implies that there falls upon such a fact something else by which it is brought low. This is what is hard and sad in necessity, immediate or abstract. The identity of the

two things, which necessity presents as bound to each other and thus bereft of their independence, is at first only inward, and therefore has no existence for those under the yoke of necessity. Freedom too from this point of view is only abstract and is preserved only by renouncing all that we immediately are and have. But, as we have seen already, the process of necessity is so directed that it overcomes the rigid externality which it first had and reveals its inward nature. It then appears that the members, linked to one another, are not really foreign to each other, but only elements of one whole, each of them, in its connexion with the other, being, as it were, at home, and combining with itself. In this way necessity is transfigured into freedom,—not the freedom that consists in abstract negation, but freedom concrete and positive. From which we may learn what a mistake it is to regard freedom and necessity as mutually exclusive. Necessity indeed *qua* necessity is far from being freedom: yet freedom presupposes necessity, and contains it as an unsubstantial element in itself. A good man is aware that the tenor of his conduct is essentially obligatory and necessary. But this consciousness is so far from making any abatement from his freedom, that without it real and reasonable freedom could not be distinguished from arbitrary choice, — a freedom which has no reality and is merely potential. A criminal, when punished, may look upon his punishment as a restriction of his freedom. Really the punishment is not foreign constraint to which he is subjected, but the manifestation of his own act: and if he recognizes this, he comports himself as a free man. In short, man is most independent when he knows himself to be determined by the absolute idea throughout.[59]

Put thus, Hegel's theory of criminal responsibility is an aspect of his idealistic history of humanity, perhaps in part as worked out in the *Phänomenologie*. There we may repeatedly perceive the struggle between the actuality of social necessity or of alienation, existing independently of human consciousness, but negated or alienated through such necessity itself, and becoming historical freedom or new social being. When Hegel's theory of abstract law or abstract necessity is understood as a theory of concrete social law, as a theory of real rather than of abstract law, he must be understood as saying that historical freedom can only be realized in and through the necessity of actual social history.

This Hegelian conception of law and state reposes first of all on the principal idea established by the *Phénoménologie de l'esprit* [writes Garaudy], that there is nothing in social life, which is not the work of man, product of his labor, of his struggles, of his thought. . . . The world of man is the work of man. There is nothing in this world of man which is inaccessible to human reason. Such are the first two dominant theses of the *Phénoménologie*. The third is the idea of alienation. These institutions created by man, these riches, this state may appear to him as things. Not as a product, but as a given. The fourth idea of the *Phénoménologie* is that the liberty of man consists in surmounting this alienation. . . . Authentic liberty can only be conquered in society and not outside it.[60]

Although Hegel's theory of human freedom as the negation of social necessity is an historical theory of social responsibility, in the *Rechtsphilosophie* this appears, as has been said, as a theory of responsibility to abstract or bourgeois criminal law. But Hegel here seems formalistic. He immediately relates such criminal law to violation of private property, and essentially explains criminal law as aggression against it. He does this in the realm of the unhistoric law of legal positivism. He resorts to the abstractness for which he had elsewhere condemned stoicism and Kant.[61] Hegel should have considered law, criminal and otherwise, after he had treated of civil society and of the state, that is, near the end and not at the beginning of the *Rechtsphilosophie*. His legal ideas in this book are abstract and not really concrete because he studies civil society and the state after he treats of abstract law, though, as has been said, he may have done this in part in order to justify (as against feudal arbitrariness) bourgeois ideas of the hegemony of law over feudal morality, as stated by Diderot. This will appear in the nineteenth century as the idea of the rule of law.

Thus it was possible for Hegel to consider abstract crime as violation of abstract property. By separating abstract property from civil society and the state, Hegel can relate the criminal law to bourgeois property in a German state which seems feudal and is not yet bourgeois. Marx shows it is not abstract law but Hegel's state which justifies feudal primogeniture;[62] other property, that is, bourgeois property, remains within the realm of abstract law. Hegel does not truly explain the relation of the state to bourgeois private property. Because appropriative alienation, that is, state alienation, is so important in Hegel's Hellenizing social theory, and because the alienation must be therefore concealed or mystified, Hegel relates bourgeois property and criminal responsibility to abstract law rather than to the state.

Ergo, he can create and justify the state, in accordance with other possibilities of objective idealism. This may be seen in his discussion of the state of Louis XIV. Here the language or heroism of flattery creates the state power of the feudal unlimited monarch,[63] in which wealth passes ". . . into the condition of relinquishing its power."[64] This is an idealistic reversal of Diderot's materialistic conception of the formation of the state. Diderot said that property is: ". . . the right that each of the individuals of which a civil society is composed has over the property which he has legitimately acquired." This requires, Diderot says, that social sacrifices be made in order to assure the tranquil possession of such property. Then Diderot says that men,

> . . . never have pretended to give [their sovereigns] an absolute and unlimited power over their property. . . . The flattery of courtiers, to whom the most absurd principles cost nothing, have sometimes persuaded some princes that they had absolute rights over the property of their subjects. . . . In states which follow the rules of reason the *properties* of private persons are under the protection of the laws. . . .[65]

Marx also writes of the

> . . . power of *abstract private property* over *the political state* [saying that] Hegel represents primogeniture as *the power of the political state over private property*. He makes of the cause the effect and of the effect the cause, of the determining the determined, and of the determined the determining.[66]

However, although Hegel reverses Diderot's materialistic conception of the feudal state, Hegel perceives what Diderot does not: The ensuing social forces in Hegel's feudal state confront each other antagonistically as the noble and as the base. Because the base consciousness is an alienated—or dishonorable, or infamed—consciousness, the Fifth Amendment of the Constitution of the United States becomes important. As it requires grand jury indictment for a formulated "infamous" crime and jury conviction, it reflects the hostility of Beccaria and of the bourgeois Enlightenment as a whole to state-imposed infamy or base-ness, such as has developed in the United States since World War II. Beccaria's hostility to the penalty of death and to infamy are both aspects of the anger of the Enlightenment against feudal criminal law. The majority of the Supreme Court of the United States has not acknowledged this, although Hobbes, even before Beccaria and Hegel, had discussed, among others, the two punishments of death and of "ignominy." If the punishment of death is punishment because it physically destroys the criminal subject of law, the punishment of infamy is punishment because it destroys the social relations of the criminal subject of law. Infamy deprives the criminal subject of law of the complex of social relations which is his being. Infamy makes the concrete or real subject of law an abstract or formal or alienated subject of law.

Assuming that Hegel does begin with real, undivided, concrete man, not with unreal no-man, not with entirely abstract man, not with man as a thing-in-itself, not with Sartre's man as empty *pour soi,* Hyppolite shows the negations through which Hegel accomplishes alienation. In Hegel's *Der Geist des Christentums und sein Schicksal,* Hyppolite says: ". . . the destiny of an individual, the destiny of a people, are the revelation of this pathos in history. Destiny is that which man is; it is his own life, his own pathos, but which appears to him as being estranged; 'destiny' Hegel profoundly writes, 'is the consciousness of myself but as an enemy.' It is by action that I thus separate myself from myself and that I find myself opposed to myself. 'Only a stone may be innocent' because it does not act; but man must act."[67] As has already been shown, Hyppolite is here explaining responsibility through reification. My reified will or destiny is my necessity, which I must alienate.

Turning to the thought of Hegel relative to modern history, it appears freedom is historical, mediated, and active, or as Garaudy says of Marxist theory, ". . . liberty is not . . . an immobile essence, congealed, given once and for all."[68] This freedom for Hegel is realized through the state. In accepting the state I accept my freedom. I accept the state through culture, or *Bildung,* or education. Hyppolite says of Hegel's considerations on the French Revolution:

The identity of the private will and the general will, of the individual and the state, therefore cannot be established immediately as it was in the ancient world, but a mediation is necessary; it rests true that liberty is for the individual to elevate himself to the general will. . . . [T]he state for Hegel is nothing artificial, it is reason on earth, but this elevation, this liberation, is no longer immediate; there is a conflict, latent or manifested, according to the case, and the modern state comprehends at once the opposition of the individual and of the general will as their reconciliation.[69]

In the bourgeois state, founded on private property, this "reconciliation" can be achieved only by alienation of the private or particular will. Though Hyppolite does not say this, he quotes Hegel as saying: *"The state is a ruse."*[70] "This note of Hegel in his course of 1805-1806," Hyppolite adds, "shows well the new conception which he has made of the state. The opposition of the particular will and the general will, of the subjective will and the objective will, is only a moment which must be transcended effectively, but which cannot take place as immediately as in the ancient city. The state is therefore the ruse which in leaving individuals alone attains all in the very play of their liberties."[71]

However, although the state is a ruse or the cunning of history, this does not yet truly explain the bourgeois criminal will, which through appropriative alienation, requires its own punishment. The relation which really unites the private and general will, necessity and freedom, is culture (or education in a very broad sense of the word).

Private individuals are therefore opposed to the universal, to the State [Hyppolite writes]. Taken as an aggregate, as vulgar, a people is still without culture, it has need to be educated, led to a sense of the universal which expresses true liberty. But it does not possess this sense immediately; it must be acquired. This is why from 1805 Hegel criticized the theory of social contract of Rousseau, or at least gave it a new meaning. The constitution of the state was represented as a free accord of particular wills. [This, too, was the thought of Beccaria.] Each alienates his 'natural liberty,' [Hyppolite continues], and it is by this alienation that the general will is formed; only, remarks Hegel, this alienation is not accomplished by itself. The private man does not also renounce easily what he considers, wrongly besides, as his liberty. . . . The

general will therefore exists *en soi.* Precisely, it is necessary that
it pass from the *en soi* to the *pour soi;* it is necessary that it
become effective. . . . [T]he general will appears to private
men as will which seems strange to them. . . . The alienation of
nature of which Rousseau speaks is only effectuated by the inter-
mediary of an historic process which Hegel calls *culture.* In the
history of states there are some moments where the state is founded
or preserved by great men who incarnate the general will an
instant and who impose it on the people despite them. . . . [T]hey
obey him against their will. It is against their will that his will is their
will. . . .[72]

In his impressive discussion of Hegel's theory of culture in his
Genèse et structure de la Phénoménologie de l'esprit de Hegel,
Hyppolite writes: "The spiritual world is the world of culture
(Bildung) and of alienation. . . . But the two terms *culture* and
alienation have a signification very close to each other."[73]

In the United States in recent years, a theory of appropriative
alienation also has been advanced by Talcott Parsons. His alienation ideas derive from idealistic value theory of neo-Kantianism:

[T]he . . . 'grounding' of a personal value is in the social
context, the network of rights and obligations which the sharing
or nonsharing of his values with others implies. The context, so
far as it involves values which can be said to be *common* to the
members of a social system, I would like to call the *legitimation*
of social action. Legitimation in this sense is the *appraisal of action
in terms of shared or common values in the context of the involve-
ment of the action in the social system.* . . . As I see it, legitimation
is the primary link between values as an internalized component
of the personality of the individual, and the institutionalized patterns
which define the structure of social relations. . . . The *functions*
of legitimation are here defined with reference to the pattern of
values itself. The process of legitimation is the bridge by which
values are joined to the differentiated subsystems of action and the
situations in which action takes place, looked at from the point
of view of the degree to which, and the mechanisms by which, the
values can be understood to play a part in the empirical regulation
of action.[74]

Garaudy seems to suggest that Hegel may have felt that his
attempt to Hellenize the bourgeois world on a higher level was
utopian.[75] It was invalid in so far as it was founded on appropriative
alienation. Hegel's theory of criminal responsibility fails with his

general theory. However, as has been said, what remains is valuable. This is Hegel's theory of historical necessity as freedom. The revolutions of the twentieth century have developed from such ideas of historical responsibility. The civil disobedience movements rest on this principle and in international criminal law, arising out of the Nürnberg Charter, the defense of compliance with superior order is not admitted. But the impact of such theory of historical responsibility has in general not yet been acknowledged.

It will be recalled that Beccaria, in general, condemned the penalty of death for crime, and that Hegel also applauded the diminished role of this penalty. In part, what Hegel criticized was Beccaria's unmediated social contract theory, whereas Hegel himself justified mediation or historical negativity. In the United States, Edward Livingston developed Beccaria's attack on capital punishment. Moreover, in effect, Livingston also touched Hegel's theory of criminal law. If, with Hegel, the punishment is due because the criminal has willed his punishment by abstract criminal law, Livingston questions the validity of the social base of the abstract criminal law. If in the *Rechtsphilosophie* Hegel sought to justify the necessity of social alienation, Livingston sought the social alienation of necessity. Livingston would not grant that the abstract or positive criminal law should protect abstract or positive property. As he believed that criminality was probably the result of unemployment, it is not difficult to develop this to mean that criminality was the result of appropriative alienation or private property. Thus Livingston overcomes Hegel, his historic contemporary. With Hegel, criminality was the attempted negation of the subjective right of private property. With Livingston, as developed, social property relations would be the negation of criminality. Of course Livingston does not say this. But at a time in the early nineteenth century when it was still difficult to find a word to express unemployment in various modern languages, Livingston perceived that the freedom of the criminal which was to be realized through the necessity of the criminal law might be a necessity to be a criminal. In his report to the Louisiana legislature on the penal *projets* Livingston said, "Everywhere, with but few exceptions, the interests of the many has, from the earliest ages, been sacrificed to the power of the few. Everywhere penal laws have been framed to support this power. . . ."[76]

Livingston's ideas of a criminal code contained a scheme of self-support for the unemployed. Perhaps this was inspired by statements in the declarations of rights formulated in France during the eighteenth century that there was a right to work. Livingston said: ". . . public education had been found to be one of the best means of preventing crimes." Then he went beyond this.

> Political society owes perfect protection to all its members in their persons, reputations and property; and it also owes necessary subsistence to those who cannot procure it for themselves. Penal laws to suppress offences are the consequences of the first obligation, those for the relief of pauperism of the second. . . . This relief must be given by providing means of employment for the industrious and gratuitous support for the helpless.[77]

This recalls what Marx and Engels said of Hegel's theory of criminal punishment: "[U]nder *human* conditions punishment will *really* be nothing but the sentence passed by the culprit on himself. There will be no attempt to persuade him that *violence* from *without,* exerted on him by others, is violence exerted on himself by himself. On the contrary he will see in *other* men his natural saviours from the sentence which he has pronounced on himself; in other words, the relation will be reversed."[78]

In part, Livingston justifies himself by developing Beccaria's idea of the import of the social contract in criminal law.

> That society owes protection to all its members is not denied. But what is that protection? Certainly its chief object is life; but whether life be assailed by the sword or by famine it is equally important. [There] are mutual obligations between society and the members who compose it, which are not written covenants; they result from the nature of the connexion, from the object to be attained by the association, which is the protection of life and property. But the preservation of life is the first object, property is only a secondary one. . . .
> . . . [A]nd if a contract is to be supposed, can it be imagined to be of a nature that would impose on any one of the contracting parties the loss of that which it was the chief end of the contract to preserve. . . ? In other words, can it be supposed that any just contract could stipulate that one of the contracting parties should die of hunger, in order that the others might enjoy, without deduction, the whole of their property?[79]

Livingston seems not only to have developed Beccaria's theory of the criminal law, but also that of Holbach. The entire Enlightenment seems to culminate in Holbach's *Le Système de nature,* published in 1770. Holbach contributes the suggestion that infliction of criminal punishment may be the unjustified consequence of faulty education or existence in a repressive state.

> . . . [I]f each society, less partial, bestowed on its members the care, the education, and the assistance which they have the right to expect, if governments less covetous and more vigilant, were sedulous to render their subjects more happy, there would not be seen such numbers of malefactors. . . . [T]hey would not be obliged to destroy life in order to punish a wickedness which is commonly ascribable to the vices of their own institutions. . . .[80]

Here Holbach's ideas as to the social cause of crime link up with the antifeudal ideas of criminal law of Beccaria and Edward Livingston.

Holbach's thinking is especially important today because of the crisis of racism in the United States, one aspect of which is a crisis in American criminal law:

Holbach pours content into Article IV, Section 4 of the Constitution, which requires the United States to guarantee a republican form of government in the particular states. In my opinion, this text justifies the removal of racist state governmental regimes by the national government and the general negation of their unconstitutional systems of criminal law.[81]

Assuming for the purpose of discussion that the Fourteenth Amendment forbids state governmental racism but tolerates private racism, this distinction collapses if such private racism is the effect of what Justice Black in his dissent in *Wilkinson v. United States* once called ". . . government by intimidation."[82] "Legal terrorism," founded on racist state interpositionism, exists today in certain states. Holbach's thought, in combination with that once advanced by Justice Black, suggests that the criminal law of such states is illegal.[83]

References

1. HEGEL, G. W. F.: *Philosophy of Right* [*Law*], T. M. KNOX (Ed.). Oxford, Clarendon Press, 1942, sec. 100.
2. *Ibid.,* sec. 99.

3. Beccaria, C. B.: *On Crimes and Punishments*, trans. by Henry Paolucci. Indianapolis, Bobbs, 1963, chap. 27.

4. D'Entrèves, in Manzoni, *The Column of Infamy*, prefaced by Cesare Beccaria's *Of Crimes and Punishment*, Foster and Grigson translation, 1964, p. xiii.

5. Franklin, M.: Sources of international law relating to sanctions against war criminals. *Journal of Criminal Law and Criminology, 36*:171, 1945-46.

6. Franklin, M.: On Hegel's theory of alienation and its historic force. *Tulane Studies in Philosophy, 9*:55, 1960.

7. *Ibid.,* p. 54.

8. Griswold v. Connecticut, 381 U. S. Rep. 479 1966. Franklin, M.: The ninth amendment as civil law method and its implications for republican form of government: Griswold v. Connecticut; South Carolina v. Katzenbach. *Tulane Law Review, 40*:496, 1966, note 16.

9. Franklin, M.: On Hegel's theory of alienation and its historic force, *op. cit.,* p. 55.

10. Cf. note 1.

11. Diderot, D.: *Interpreter of Nature, Selected Writings*, trans. by Jean Stewart and Jonathan Kemp. London, Lawrence and Wishart, 1937, pp. 146, 181.

12. Esmein, A.: *A History of Continental Criminal Procedure with Special Reference to France*, trans. by John Simpson, 1914, p. 614, note 1.

13. Chinard, G. (Ed.): *The Commonplace Book of Thomas Jefferson*, 1926, pp. 298, 304.

14. Wroth, L. K., and Zobel, H. B. (Eds): *The Legal Papers of John Adams*. Cambridge, Harvard U. P., 1965, vol. 3, p. 16, notes 28, 48, 231, 232, 242. Butterfield, L. H.: *Diary and Autobiography of John Adams*. Cambridge, Harvard U. P., 1961, vol. 3, p. 194. Adams, C. F.: *The Works of John Adams*. Boston, Little, 1850-56, vol. 2, p. 238.

15. Justice Douglas dissenting in Ullmann v. United States, 350 U. S. R. 450, 1956.

16. Hegel, *Philosophy of Right* [*Law*], *op. cit.,* sec. 100, addition.

17. *Ibid.,* sec. 62. See also section 180, attack on *fideicommissa* and *substitutions* as "infringement of the principle of the freedom of property".

18. Marx, K.: *Critique de la philosophie de l'etat de Hégel*, trans. by Molitor. In Marx, *Oeuvres philosophiques*, vol. 4, p. 205.

19. Hegel, *op. cit.,* section 90.

20. *Ibid.,* section 94.

21. *Ibid.,* section 99.

22. Cf. note 4.

23. HOLMES, O. W., JR.: *The Common Law.* Boston, Little, 1881, p. 42.
24. DYNNIK, M. (Ed.): *Geschichte der Philosophie.* Berlin, Dt. Verl. d. Wissenschaften, 1960, vol. 2, p. 93.
25. PIONTKOWSKI, A.: *Hegel's Lehre über Staat und Recht und seine Strafrechtstheorie,* trans. by Anna Neuland. Berlin, Deutscher Zentralverlag, 1960, p. 165.
26. *Ibid.*
27. MARX, K., and ENGELS, F.: *The Holy Family,* trans. by R. Dixon. Moscow, Foreign Language Publishing House, 1956. p. 238.
28. Cf. HEGEL, G. W. F.: *The Phenomenology of Mind,* 2nd ed., trans. by J. B. Baillie. New York, Macmillan, 1931, p. 82. Cf. Niel, *De la médiation dans la philosophie de Hegel,* 1945, pp. 70, 108, 112.
29. See Stiehler: Die Dialektik in Hegels *Phänomenologie des Geistes,* 1964, pp. 251, 255.
30. HEGEL, *Philosophy of Right. op. cit.,* sec. 190.
31. Cf. HEGEL, G. W. F.: *Science of Logic,* trans. by W. H. Johnston and L. G. Struthers. Humanities, 1929, vol. 1, p. 133.
32. PEPERZAK, A. T.: *Le jeune Hegel et la vision morale du monde.* La Haye, M. Nijhoff, 1960, p. 163.
33. FRANKLIN, M.: On Hegel's theory of alienation and its historic force. *op. cit.,* p. 60.
34. HEGEL, *Philosophy of Right. op. cit.,* sec. 104.
35. *Ibid.,* sec. 104, addition.
36. HEGEL, *The Phenomenology of Mind. op. cit.,* p. 395.
37. HYPPOLITE, J.: *Genèse et structure de la Phénoménologie de l'esprit de Hegel.* Paris, Aubier, 1946, p. 277.
38. HEGEL, *The Phenomenology of Mind. op. cit.,* p. 340.
39. CORNU, A.: *Karl Marx et Friedrich Engels.* Paris, Presses universitaires de France, 1955-58, vol. 3, p. 135.
40. MARX, K. *Economic and Philosophic Manuscripts of 1844,* trans. by Milligan. n.d., p. 103.
41. See Lukács, *Der junge Hegel.* Berlin, Aufbau-Veil, 1954, p. 220, note 2.
42. HEGEL, G.W.F.: The spirit of Christianity and its fate. In *On Christianity, Early Theological Writings,* trans. by T. M. Knox. Torchbook, 1961, pp. 182, 225, 226, 227, 229.
43. ROSSI, M.: *Marx e la dialettica hegeliana.* Roma Editori riuniti, 1960, vol. 1, p. 615.
44. LUKÁCS, *op. cit.,* p. 221.
45. HEGEL, *On Christianity, Early Theological Writings. op. cit.,* p. 221.
46. HEGEL an v. HENNING (?), March 19, 1825. In *Briefe von und an Hegel.* Flechsig, 1960, vol. 4, p. 25.
47. HEGEL, *op. cit.,* p. 228.
48. *Ibid.,* p. 227.

49. *Ibid.,* p. 230.
50. MARX, *Economic and Philosophic Manuscripts of 1844, op cit.,* p. 79.
51. HEGEL, *ibid.,* p. 229.
52. ROSSI, *op. cit.,* p. 615.
53. HEGEL, *The Phenomenology of Mind,* pp. 386, 399, 403, 404, 408, 409.
54. FRANKLIN, M.: Influence of the Abbé de Mably and of Le Mercier de la Rivière on American constitutional ideas concerning the Republic and judicial review. In Pound, R., Griswold and Sutherland (Eds.): *Perspectives of Law, Essays for Austin Wakeman Scott,* Boston, Little, 1964, pp. 96, 97.
55. HEGEL, *op. cit.,* p. 409.
     GARAUDY, R.: *Dieu Est Mort Etude sur Hegel.* Paris, Presses universitaires de France, 1962, p. 23.
     GRAY, R.: *Hegel's Hellenic Ideal.* New York, King's Crown Press, 1941, p. 53.
     LUKÁCS, *op. cit.,* p. 76.
     BARION, J.: *Hegel und die marxistische Staatslehre.* Bonn, Bouvier, 1963, p. 23.
56. LUKÁCS, *op. cit.,* p. 239.
     PIONTKOWSKI, *op. cit.,* pp. 95, 96, 141.
     GARAUDY, R.: *La Liberté,* 1955, p. 135.
     PEPERZAK, *op. cit.,* p. 165.
57. HYPPOLITE, J.: *Introduction à la philosophie de l'histoire de Hegel.* Paris, M. Rivière, 1948, p. 35.
58. HEGEL, *Philosophy of Right, op. cit.,* sec. 104.
59. *The Logic of Hegel,* 2nd ed., trans. by Wallace. *Encyclopaedia of the Philosophical Sciences,* 1892, p. 282.
60. GARAUDY, *Dieu est mort Etude sur Hegel. Ibid.,* p. 270.
     Cf. FOULQUIÉ, P.: *Dictionnaire de la langue philosophique.* Paris, Presses universitaires de France, 1962, p. 403.
61. FRANKLIN, M.: The significance of stoicism in Roman law in the development and outcome of Hegel's theory of alienation. *Acta Juridica,* 1958, pp. 246-47.
62. MARX, *Oeuvres Philosophiques, loc. sit.*
63. HEGEL, G. W. F.: *La Phenoménologie de l'esprit,* trans. by Jean Hyppolite. 1947, vol. 2, p. 72.
64. HEGEL, *The Phenomenology of Mind, op cit.* p. 535.
65. DIDEROT, D.: Propriété. In *Oeuvres de Denis Diderot.* Paris, J.L.J. Brière, 1821-1834, vol. 18, pp. 501, 502.
66. MARX, *loc. cit.*
67. HYPPOLITE, *Introduction à la philosophie de l'histoire de Hegel. op. cit.,* p. 270.
68. GARAUDY, *La Liberté,* p. 135.
69. *Ibid.,* p. 83.

70. HYPPOLITE, *op. cit.,* p. 85.
71. *Ibid.*
72. *Ibid.,* p. 87.
73. HYPPOLITE, *Genèse et Structure de la Phenoménologie de l'esprit de Hegel, op. cit.,* p. 371.
74. PARSONS, T.: Authority, legitimation, and social action. Friedrich, C. J. (Ed.): *Authority,* Cambridge, Harvard U. P. 1958, p. 204.
75. GARAUDY, *Dieu est mort Etude sur Hegel, op. cit.,* p. 262.
76. FRANKLIN, M.: Concerning the historic importance of Edward Livingston. *Tulane Law Review,* 11:207, 1937.
77. *Ibid.*
78. MARX and ENGELS, *The Holy Family, op. cit.,* p. 238.
79. FRANKLIN, *ibid.,* p. 208.
80. HOLBACH, *The System of Nature* [1770], trans. by Robinson, 1868, vol. 1, p. 132.
81. FRANKLIN, M.: Interposition Interposed: II. *Law in Transition,* vol. 21, p. 90.
    FRANKLIN, M.: Concerning the influence of Roman law on the formulation of the Constitution of the United States. *Tulane Law Review,* 38:636, 1964.
82. JUSTICE BLACK dissenting in Wilkinson v. United States, 81 S. Ct. Rep. p. 579, 1961.
83. Cf. note 81, p. 92, note 131.

COMMENTS
J. D. Hyman

I take the title of Professor Franklin's paper to imply that there is a general theory which will materially further our understanding of the problems involved in organized society's age-old practice of formally inflicting punishment. And I assume that in the present context "punishment" means the intentional infliction of pain or deprivation upon a person because he has violated the command of a criminal law. If that is the meaning of the title, then I find that the paper does not persuade me that the writers discussed make a major contribution to such a general theory.

I understand the argument of the paper to run as follows. Hegel, like Beccaria, addressed himself to the central ethical problem of punishment: If the infliction of pain upon others is an evil, how can society justify the systematic infliction of pain upon some of its members? The dilemma is altogether avoided if the criminal to be punished, himself wills that the punishment be inflicted upon himself. The punishment is in fact willed by the society of which the criminal is a part. Therefore, if the criminal shares the general will which wills that punishment, he wills his own punishment and it ceases to be the infliction of pain upon another.

Basically, the paper is a search in Hegel's writings for a sound conceptual basis for making criminal punishment by society self-determined, as Hegel and Beccaria believed it should be. I am sympathetic to the principle that in all of man's relations with other men, each should be treated as subject, not object. In his recent book, *The Broken Image,* to which I will refer later, Professor Floyd Matson quotes a summary of Martin Buber's expression of this distinction which to me seems apt:

> The *I-Thou* points to a relation of person to person, of subject to subject, a relation of reciprocity involving 'meeting' or 'encounter', while the *I-It* points to a relation of person to thing, of subject to object, involving some form of utilization, domination, or control, even if it is only so-called 'objective' knowing.[1]

Admirable as this goal is, I am not persuaded it is substantially achievable in society's relations with its subjects through the criminal law.

My principal problem is that I believe a heavy burden of persuasion rests upon the proponent of a single proposition or principle offered as the key to the understanding of any of the major problems of human affairs. Matson, in the book previously referred to, propounds the thesis that the proper study of man and society demands a perspective which treats man as a whole and recognizes his volitional impact upon the physical, biological, psychological, and social forces which impinge upon him. He relies heavily, as a first step in his argument, upon the views of physical scientists who have rejected efforts to reduce knowledge of the physical world to a rigidly precise space-time-force pattern, and have postulated indeterminacy in the very structure of the universe and of life. Matson then argues that depth psychology and social science must *a fortiori* accept a total approach to individual man as a starting point along with the element of indeterminacy which results. This position not only rejects reductionism and rigid determinism, but also challenges the adequacy of highly generalized conceptions to yield an understanding of man as individual and in his social relations. He quotes de Broglie on the point that the concepts produced by the human mind are ". . . roughly valid for reality . . ." so long as they are formulated in slightly vague fashion but that ". . . when extreme precision is aimed at, they become ideal forms whose content tends to vanish away."[2]

Similarly, I find this tendency in the spinning out of Hegel's concepts of alienation and its rejection through the resolution of freedom and necessity in the historical state. I doubt such abstractions can significantly illuminate the problems of punishment of criminal conduct in modern society. Specifically, observation indicates that individuals in society confront the criminal law's prescriptions and punishments with such widely varying attitudes as to preclude any reasonable expectation that a single hypothesis about the reconciliation between the individual and the general will can comprehend the full range of attitudes and the reactions which they engender.

To a considerable degree, those who are educated within a given culture appear to accept its formally promulgated norms as appropriate and just most of the time; in this sense they can be said to will their own punishment for transgressing those norms. But to the extent that punishment by society serves other goals than fulfilling the criminal's will, he becomes *pro tanto* an object. And the evidence is compelling that other goals always have been and will continue to be served. One relevant item is that the occasions for, and the measure of, punishment are determined by society with at least one eye on deterrence.[3]

Under conditions which negate the likelihood that punishment will have a deterrent effect, organized society seems customarily to have punished wrongdoers in order to discourage the vengeful resort to force by those injured or by persons closely identified with them. Psychoanalytical thought today does not lack spokesmen for the position that a vengeance-seeking response to criminal acts represents an urge so basic in human beings that the law is well-advised to take account of it in the interest of preserving public order.[4]

Another personality factor which appears to support the social imposition of punishment without regard to the will of the criminal is the need to maintain or reinforce in the community-at-large the internalized patterns which acculturation has shaped. Those who would be prepared to will their own punishment for a transgression of prescribed norms might find their will to do so weakened if they repeatedly observed similar transgressions by others going unpunished.

A related but distinct motive for punishment is to satisfy the needs of those members of society whose own forbidden impulses threaten to become uncontrollable if the criminal who yielded to such impulses is not punished.

On a different level, the pattern of life is felt to be threatened when the beliefs basic to that pattern are called in question. Society, as much in its collective interest as to protect the peace of mind of its subjects, has a long history of attempting to prevent the introduction and circulation of ideas which conflict with the prevailing pattern of beliefs.

I am suggesting that these varied reactions to deviant behavior influence (if they do not altogether determine) what society, pursuing the goals of retribution and deterrence, proscribes; the nature of the deprivations which it establishes for violations; the energy with which those deprivations are invoked. The other traditional goals of criminal law — reformation and the restraint of the criminal thought to be a continuing danger — add new dimensions of complexity.

Moreover, I find it hard to believe that any society, whatever its economic basis, will be wholly free from individuals who explicitly challenge it in some way, and, therefore, deny the propriety of the punishment it imposes. At one extreme is the personality called "psychopathic" which acknowledges no externally imposed restraints; which simply does not allow itself to be influenced, much less appropriated, by a social will. Then there is the unqualified revolutionary who finds the society wholly wrong and incorrigible in its foundations, thus requiring total uprooting and reconstruction. Neither intellectually nor emotionally does he feel a bond to it; his commitments are real, although lying beyond that society. Possibly the next category includes those who accept the society and feel themselves a part of it, but withhold their allegiance in some particulars as to which its commands or behavior are seen as violating a commitment even more fundamental. Such are the countless individuals over the centuries who justified their forbidden behavior in the light of a higher law felt to be obligatory upon them. Taking Antigone as an example, it is doubtful that she willed her punishment in any meaningful sense. Can she be regarded as anything but a defiant object? Perhaps the pure civil disobedient of today wills his punishment, acknowledging that he violates a law which is valid within the society whose basic structure he accepts, and suffering the prescribed punishment as a means of drawing attention to grave evils in that society.

What we have to work with in this field of inquiry is composed mostly of *a priori* speculations about human nature which are based upon introspection, social observation, and historical data; selective borrowings from theories of social psychology and depth psychology, and fragments of experimental and clinical evidence in these last two fields, which are accumulating with painful slowness.[5]

I do not understand how any single hypothesis about the reconciliation of individual and general will, or determinism and freedom, can provide society with a useful working principle for dealing, as it must, with the spectrum of problems only sketched above.

Hegel's broader views may or may not prove fruitful in the construction of an abstract framework upon which all of our age's knowledge about man and society may be illuminatingly arranged, a task which Whitehead believed to be one of the main functions of philosophy. Until some such large framework challenges decisively the soundness or coherence of the present selective, somewhat eclectic group of concepts with which our society approaches the problem of punishment, I believe we must continue to struggle in those terms.

Professor Franklin suggests that contemporary bourgeois social and legal theory, declining to accept the Hegelian theory of the unity of necessity and freedom through the state in history, wavers with futility between the theories of absolute necessity and absolute freedom of will; and asks, in connection with criminal law, whether the accused had the formal freedom or "intention" required for the particular crime. I do not find so polar a swing. On the one hand, I see no evidence of significant espousal in theory (there is certainly none in practice) of a notion of absolute predetermination. What is evident is a continuing debate as to where the line should be drawn to mark that deviant harmful act which is to be punished by criminal law, and that which is to be exculpated. Nor do I understand why even a strict theory of determinism would end the debate.[6] For all the reasons just mentioned, the maintenance of order in society would seem to justify the imposition of punishment when the factor of causal wish is ascertained to be present to the degree thought appropriate.

Professor Franklin touches on a few more specific aspects of criminal law in the light of the philosophy of punishment. One relates to capital punishment. Its role is shrinking in the Western world, not because of increasing acceptance of total determinism, but because of a spreading conviction that its deterrent impact is very limited and because an error in identifying the criminal is irretrievable.

I have not attempted, and I am not qualified, to determine the soundness of Professor Franklin's reinterpretation of the bearing of Hegel's thought on the fundamental problems of criminal responsibility and punishment. For reasons which I have attempted to sketch, I do not find the principle which emerges helpful either for coping with the problem of punishment for crime in a property-based society, or for encouraging the belief that the problems will disappear in a society otherwise based.

References

1. MATSON, F.: *The Broken Image*. Garden City, Anchor Books, 1966, p. 224.

2. *Ibid.*, p. 138. De Broglie also stated that whenever we undertake to describe facts, we are dealing on the one hand ". . . with a Reality which is always infinitely complex and full of an infinity of shades, and on the other with our understanding, which forms conceptions which are always more or less rigid and abstract." In later writings, de Broglie has turned away from the probability interpretation of microscopic phenomena. See his *New Perspectives in Physics* (1961), pp. vii-viii, 106, 171-76. In any event, he has not rejected the point for which he is quoted above. See his enthusiastic foreword to Bohm's *Causality and Chance in Modern Physics* (1957), and Bohm's statement at p. 156: "It is clear, then, that all our concepts are, in a great many ways, abstract representations of matter in the process of becoming." *Toward a Unified Theory of Human Behavior* (1956), pp. 38-50, includes a stimulating discussion about the problems of observation and communication of psychological and social phenomena, in which an analogy to the problems of indeterminacy and complementarity in physics is suggested.

3. NEWMAN, K. J.: Punishment and the breakdown of the legal order: The experience in East Pakistan. *Nomos,* 1960, vol. 3, p. 128.

4. SCHOENFELD, C. G.: In defense of retribution in the law, *Psychoanalytic Quarterly, 35*:108, 1966.

5. Perhaps the most concentrated body of contemporary data bearing on the uses and results of punishment is to be found in the work of the psychologists and psychiatrists who have been working on the control of behavior of rebellious and disturbed school children. A recent carefully ordered collection of studies of such work, *Conflict in the Classroom,* edited by N. J. Long, W. C. Morse, and R. G. Newman, contains an impressive amount of observational data and reports on experimental work.

6. Professor Baylis stated one basis for this claim in the present symposium. Also convincing is Joel Feinberg's recent statement that the adoption of a deterministic view does not negate the justice of punishment. He notes that men may still be regarded as the true authors of their deeds if their wish has caused the deeds, even if the wish to do the deeds was determined. Cf. Feinberg: On justifying legal punishment. *Nomos,* 1960, vol. 3, pp. 152, 166.

PUNISHMENT AND ITS MYTHOLOGICAL CONTEXT

Berkley B. Eddins

We are indebted to Professor Franklin for a richly detailed exposition and sensitively handled analysis of some of the most important developments in the theory of criminal responsibility. After commenting briefly on several points in Mr. Franklin's treatment, I shall offer some reflections on the broader issues in social philosophy some of which, of course, were mentioned in his paper.

Two theories of alienation were distinguished: alienation as appropriation, and self-alienation. Actually, there are two distinct, but related types of alienation in the former theory which might have been unwittingly compressed by Mr. Franklin. The first is when an important part of the subject willingly passes over into an object: The subject—as in the sphere of the political—alienates part of himself to the larger body; or, in ordinary activity, the artisan vests part of himself in his product. This alienation is something which is positive, nonoppressive, and is not usually looked upon as being of disvalue to the agent. In contrast to this process, there is the seizure (by another) of the human consciousness now embodied in the object-artifact, which seizure is indeed oppressive.

Mr. Franklin has shown how existentialist alienation (self-alienation) may be derivative with respect to appropriative alienation. The former may be caused by the latter. But one may also be alienated in the existentialist sense because one is prevented from (willingly) allowing part of one's consciousness to pass over into an object—in this case, certain political and social institutions and activities. Nothing has been seized because nothing has been given over; yet there is "alienation." (We may note, in passing, that the basic meaning of "alienation" is "estrangement from reality or from meaningful activity.") If this is plausible, then the criticism of Sartre does not hold because there can be alienation without seizure. Sartre does not need an appropriative theory of alienation, but there may be real and meaningful alienation apart from, and independent of, alienation of the appropriative type.

Mr. Franklin has asserted that even Sartre's *pour soi* may indeed will its own punishment. It would be enlightening to know what the nature of that punishment would be, and what the (social) agents or instruments of that punishment would be. It is not quite clear, moreover, that for the reason given by Mr. Franklin (i.e., that even Sartre's man is not a nothing), a Sartrean theory of criminality would still be a theory of *appropriative* alienation. It is one thing to say a person is a complex of historic social relations, yet another to say he has so related to his society—that he has allowed or caused a part of his consciousness to pass over into the objects, artifacts, or institutions of that society.

Turning to another matter, briefly, although the point about Hegel's criticism of (Rousseau's) contract theory is well-taken, it might be misleading not to mention the emphases (also in Rousseau) on freedom as moral self-control, the educative effects of participating in decisions of sovereignty, and the extent to which a man could be "forced to be free." Rousseau's man also is the civilized man, the product of culture and refinement, having come to recognize the general will as his own. (There are, however, important differences betwen Hegel and Rousseau which cannot be gainsaid.)

Mr. Franklin's characterization of the Enlightenment emphasis on the educative function of bourgeois law (and, I might add, of social institutions) is generally accurate. The passage quoted from Diderot's *Supplement to Bougainville's Voyage* does seem to bring Diderot quite close to the social and institutional determinism of Helvétius' *Treatise on Man*. But Diderot differs from Helvétius in rejecting Helvétius' views that: (1) justice was simply conformity to the nation's laws . . . (2) without laws men could have no idea of justice. Diderot held, in *James the Fatalist* and in the *Refutation of Helvétius,* that man not only had free will, but also a conscience and a basic idea of justice prior to the formation of the social contract. Diderot, moreover, by admitting the passions as part of man's original makeup, provides for individuality, freedom, and dynamism not allowable on Helvétius' reductive sensationalism and institutional determinism. This determinism (metaphysical and social) is also characteristic of D'Holbach's *System of Nature*. Here again, while Diderot would agree with the importance of education respecting the more general *desiderata,* he would have to reject the deterministic cast of D'Holbach's views.

With respect to Mr. Franklin's treatment of Hegel, it might be well for him to place special emphasis upon the fact that while Hegel starts with abstract law (and hence, has trouble reconciling the individual will to the universal will) nevertheless, by the time Hegel has worked out his complete view of the state, society, and education, he does then possess the machinery for reconciling these wills. I do not see that Mr. Franklin has to follow Justice Holmes' position that there is an unbridgeable scission, even on Hegel's complete view, between individual and society.

Hegel's theory of criminal responsibility has, among others, the following valuable features:

1. It treats the criminal as *subject,* and not as *object* of his punishment
2. By bringing in the universal will, he avoids the "ad hoc" quality of strictly utilitarian theories
3. It shows the importance of social institutions in the development of the legitimation of punishment.

To be sure, his whole theory of punishment is based upon a theory of history, a theory of man and society, a system of idealistic philosophy. But what bothers me most of all is that he seems to rely on a mainly mythological characterization of human activity, although it is a beautiful one. (I take the chief function of a myth to be that of being suggestive of a likely way of looking at things, or of being economical in summing up common conceptions concerning phenomena.) And is seems no matter how "scientific" or enlightened we become about various aspects of the theory and practice of punishment, its basic rationale remains on the mythological level. Whether we hold to punishment as retribution, rehabilitation, deterrence, or "social surgery," we do not escape the mythological. A dominant, but by no means exclusive myth has been, and still is, that ". . . imbalance must be redressed, order must be restored, the gods must be appeased." Actually, what bothers me is not that the rationales have been, might be, or must be, mythological; rather, it is that we have not thought about guidelines for formulating an adequate myth, or for judging one to be so. What rationale will provide for a theory which is philosophically sound, historically in focus, in keeping with our latest (empirical) scientific theories, and yet will be just, moral, and soul-satisfying?

I think there are broader issues in social philosophy involved in the theory of punishment. We cannot expect to have an adequate theory of punishment unless and until we have an adequate theory of what human activity is all about. In other words, we need a good myth, or some good myths. If we want a theory of punishment where:

(a) The criminal is subject and not object,

(b) The severity of punishment is proportional to the gravity of the crime,

(c) The rule of law is observed,

(d) Punishment is legitimated by being related to the educative offices of the institutions of the society or culture,

then we must see to it that we have a certain kind of social philosophy and a certain kind of human *praxis*.

Now, having made this contention, I am not going to spell out in detail what such a social philosophy would be. But, echoing Mr. Franklin's final point, and expanding it somewhat, I would like to make the following observation: Not only may the criminal law in some states in the United States be illegal, but it might be the case that under certain social systems, especially those which do not provide for economic as well as political democracy, where there is neither social cohesion, national direction, nor real political education, much of criminal law may be morally indefensible.

REPLY TO
COMMENTS

MITCHELL FRANKLIN

I am grateful for the careful and thoughtful remarks prepared by Professor Eddins and Professor Hyman in connection with my paper.

Professor Hyman advances several ideas which I should consider. His discussion of my presentation of Hegel's theory of self-determined criminal punishment must be mentioned. I criticized Hegel's theory of self-determined criminal responsibility because Hegel cannot make the transition from the particular will of the criminal to the general criminal law of the state without seizing, or appropriating, or alienating the will of the criminal; thus, attributing also to the criminal subject of law the will to be punished by the criminal law of the state. As the criminal has indeed willed his criminal act as a particular or private will, his alienated, or reified, or "fetishized" will confronts him as his own enemy, though Hegel said this general will is his own will. Although Hegel's criminal appears as a subject of law, this subject of law is veered by Hegel, so that he becomes the object of such law and the general, reified will becomes the subject of law.

I said that Hegel's theory of self-determined criminality in truth was an appropriative alienation theory of criminal responsibility because it was a bourgeois theory of criminal law. Because bourgeois society is founded on appropriative alienation or on private property in the means of production, bourgeois criminal law also could occupy or alienate the will of the criminal. Hegel's own considerations relating to Leibniz' theory of ground (if ground or infrastructure is understood as social ground) may be mentioned here to contradict Hegel's own abstract or formal theory of self-determined criminal punishment. Heidegger would reject my conception of ground.

Hegel's theory of self-determined criminal responsibility ceases to be an alienation theory if there is no alienation in the structure of society. Professor Hyman is not persuaded of this. Indeed, he seems to believe that the self-determination of the criminal enjoys, or should enjoy, no role in the criminal law of any form of social organization. But there may be some justification in legal history for Hegel's theory of self-determined, legal responsibility. As the body of my paper shows, both Beccaria and Livingston invoke the social contract in their theory of criminal law. Of course, such theory is discredited by Hegel himself. However, it has been mentioned that in kin-organized Rome, preceding the history of private property relations, competence to make determination was willed through a preliminary procedural contract *(litis contestatio)*. This at first was a self-determined submission to an arbitral process. Even until this decade of the twentieth century, Article 162 of the old Romanist Louisiana Code of Civil Procedure stated the general principle that the subject of law should be tried before ". . . his own judge *(son propre juge)*." This developed out of the history of Roman law. This concept is preserved today in the power of each of the permanent members of the Security Council of the United Nations to condemn itself. This is called "the unanimity principle." In feudal English law a division developed in legal power between the common law as such and equity. In equity, it was pretended that the wrong-doer, for religious or natural law reasons, would himself determine to do what his conscience, as stated in the determination of the chancellor or equity judge, suggested.[1] Hegel at length considers the theory of self-determined responsibility in writing of the trial of Socrates. Here Hegel defends the principle of self-determined punishment; but in criticizing Socrates shows that his theory, insofar as it concerns the bourgeois state, is an appropriative alienation theory.[2]

Professor Hyman perhaps has not mastered the purport of my discussion of freedom and necessity, which Hegel derived from his theory of self-determined criminality. What must be repeated is that because of historical necessity there may be a self-determined responsibility to oppose the positive criminal law *in vigor* in the state, accepting the criminal consequences thereof. In the words of Lucien Sève, I may have a responsibility to change what I can change.[3] In my text, I mentioned that this historical responsibility to confront the positive criminal law is now acknowledged in Second World War texts, which deny the defense of adherence to superior order.

Professor Hyman seems to maintain that appropriative alienation is not merely bourgeois, but is eternal or permanent. (This, too, I may say, was the view of Max Weber.) Professor Hyman says there is ". . . a heavy burden of persuasion . . . upon the proponent of a single proposition or principle offered as the key to understanding of any of the major problems of human affairs." He thus makes his contribution to a dialogue which has been proceeding at least since the time of the *abbé* de Mably at the close of the Enlightenment, and which culminates in Marx and Engels. I certainly agree with Professor Hyman that the theory of the role of appropriative alienation cannot be determined without making fine scientific discriminations. For instance, I may add to my paper that Hegel, in his discussion of the role of labor in the relation of master and slave, shows that the master who appropriates or alienates the labor of the slave may be himself alienated by the slave.[4] Shargorodskii writes:

> Analysis of crime in modern capitalist society shows that a vast
> number of crimes are committed by persons who are not of the

laboring classes at all. . . . Everything that is most characteristic and typical of crime in modern bourgeois society is rooted in the contemporary societal relations of capitalism, and not in need alone. Crime in modern capitalist society is born primarily out of the striving for maximum profit.[5]

In brief confrontations, such as this occasion, it is necessary to present and hold firmly to basic ideas. Hence I shall terminate my considerations of this aspect of the critique of Professor Hyman by reiterating my thought that present-day criminality must be related to the role of appropriative alienation in bourgeois society, and in bourgeois society alone. Professor John Lekschas, director of the Institute of Criminal Law, Humboldt University, Berlin, and Professor Richard Hartmann, department of criminal law at the same university, write in a recent essay:

From present-day criminological literature we know of many attempts to explain the causes of criminality. All these attempts are successful to a certain extent in finding an explanation for the phenomenon of crime. However, we share Sheldon Glueck's opinion that in all these theories, certain aspects are overemphasized, resulting in a narrow approach. Criminology which deals with human conduct must necessarily be based on the laws of human society. We regard as rather unfruitful to base criminological research on the individual only, as is sometimes recommended. . . . The social essence of criminality lies in the protest or raging of the isolated individual or whole groups against dominating situations, conditions, of life or the social system.[6]

In their paper, "Social Foundations and Forms of Organization of the Fight for the Gradual Suppression of Criminality in the GDR," Professor Joachim Renneberg of the criminal law department and deputy chairman of the Institute of Political Science and Jurisprudence, Potsdam-Babelsberg, and Dr. Walter Krutzch, scientific assistant in the Ministry of Justice, report that by 1964 recorded crime had dropped in the GDR to 27.6 percent as compared with 1946.[7]

In opposing my conception that modern criminality develops out of bourgeois social relations, Professor Hyman defends ". . . the present selective, somewhat eclectic group of concepts with which our society approaches the problem of punishment. . . ." I should like to invite Professor Hyman to consider whether through

Hegel's theory of mediation, certain strains of thought presented in his eclecticism might yield a unity such as I have indicated. Through mediation, a new immediacy might emerge which would resolve the differences between his thought and mine. Here, I like to mention the damage which Professor Friedrich does to the development of American social thought when he suggests that Hegel's negations express, not relations and connections, but annihilations and destructions.[8]

Professor Hyman's choice of sources for his eclecticism seems arbitrary. Although he is a jurist, he says: "I have not attempted, and I am not qualified, to determine the soundness of Professor Franklin's reinterpretation of the bearing of Hegel's thought on the fundamental problems of criminal responsibility and punishment." Nevertheless, the *Rechtsphilosophie,* the summary title of the volume in which Hegel states his theory of criminal law, should be translated "Philosophy of Law,"[9] and is within the competence of jurists. Profesor Hyman should not have been intimidated from an encounter with Hegel merely because the summary title of Hegel's work has been mistranslated as "philosophy of right" (Dyde, Knox) or "philosophy of right and law" (Friedrich). But Professor Hyman does not hesitate to venture into the realm of "psychoanalytical thought."

Moreover, Professor Hyman at some length postulates ". . . indeterminacy in the very structure of the universe and of life . . .," thus condemning some aspects of my paper. I am not competent to pursue Professor Hyman into the world of physical science, although I know certain of the philosophical discussions which have centered about the so-called principle of indeterminacy. I am encouraged because Reichenbach has related the ". . . epistemological analysis of quantum physics . . ." to Hume, saying that ". . . nothing essential has been added to his discovery."[10] And Bernal concludes:

> Actually the construction put on the quantum theory is altogether arbitrary and uncalled for. . . . Even if it were true on the atomic level it would not justify all its extension to the fields of the far more complicated biological and social levels.[11]

Even during the early period in which Eddington writes, Margenau maintained that quantum theory comes to the rescue of the causality principle.[12]

I may add to these considerations relative to the so-called indeterminacy principle Professor Reck's presentation of the dialectical thought of Professor Blanshard, who has taken part in these proceedings devoted to the theory of punishment:

> Blanshard's fifth argument for the internality of relations rests upon his extraordinary theory of causality. He argues: '(1) that all things are *causally* related, directly or indirectly; (2) that being causally related involves being *logically* related. . . .' Causality is for Blanshard a cardinal postulate of science and rational investigation, and although recent physics has cast doubt on the indispensability and the validity of this postulate, Blanshard takes pains to allay these doubts by showing that such developments as the Heisenberg principle of indeterminacy are methodological only and do not touch upon the causal relatedness of reality. But more than this, Blanshard strives to equate causal relatedness with logical relatedness. [After some further discussion, Professor Reck says of Professor Blanshard's dialectical outlook:] Causality itself illustrates the internality of relations.[13]

I am pleased that Professor Eddins accepted my theory of the role of Article IV, Section 4 of the Constitution, requiring the United States to guarantee republican form of government within the particular states. He sees the possibilities of that particular part of the Constitution as a weapon against racism in Southern and other states. This constitutional text does not have an English origin, but perhaps sums up the social and legal theory of the French Enlightenment. Montesquieu had said that the principle of monarchies (or of feudalism) was honor; and that the principle of republics (or of the bourgeois world) was virtue. Article IV, Section 4 of the Constitution requires the introduction or maintenance of such republican virtue in the United States. For Helvétius, Diderot and Holbach, Montesquieu's theory of republican virtue seemed to solve the problem of feudal alienation. These mechanistic thinkers believed feudal alienation could be ended through education; the supreme act of education being the act of legislation, and, in private law, of codification, through which a rational lawmaker would educate or create the enlightened or virtuous citizen and thus end feudal or irrational alienation. As the American law school world and the Government of the United States, in its totality, have refused to recognize and to invoke the possibilities of Article IV, Section 4, one may question whether there has been good faith in the struggle against American racism and American interpositionism.

I was enchanted by Professor Eddins' response to my paper because of his discussion of the theory of alienation, and because of his interest in my reference to Sartre. I should like to reiterate that appropriative alienation of labor is reflected as superstructural or cultural-political, appropriative alienation, and as fetishism or reification, which is related to appropriative alienation. Hegel himself addresses himself to the alienation not only of labor, but also of language. However, Hegel may fail to distinguish "exteriorization" or human *praxis* from appropriative alienation. I believe that this is the view of both Hyppolite and Cornu.

Professor Eddins suggests that my theory of appropriative alienation may fail ". . . because one is prevented from (willingly) allowing part of one's consciousness to pass over into an object—in this case, certain political and social institutions and activities. Nothing has been seized because nothing has been given over; yet there is 'alienation.' " Because appropriative alienation takes the form of private property in bourgeois society, I think Professor Eddins' criticism may be answered. The essence of private property is its exclusiveness. And as the bourgeois state guarantees this exclusiveness, it seems to me that the worker who works for wages and the worker who is excluded from work, for instance, for racial reasons, have both been appropriated by the bourgeois state.

It is a pity that Sartre has to be considered so late in this conference. In my essay I described Sartre's *pour soi* as a ". . . remote kinsman . . ." of Hegel's bourgeois criminal because both appear only as in-themselves. Hence, as both begin without concrete, historical social relations, they are nothings. It is true Hegel's *Rechtsphilosophie* gives a magnificent account of social relations, but before these relations are fully developed, the abstract human being already may have become a bourgeois criminal. As my essay indicates, Hegel himself calls his criminal a "person." The word "person" or *persona* suggests perhaps that because the bourgeois criminal may not yet have the concrete, many-sided social relations he possesses toward the end of the *Rechtsphilosophie,* Hegel's criminal "person" may be only a mask concealing a nothing.

Sartre's early *pour soi* seems to me to be nothing. But within the subsequent development of Sartre's thought he also advances a theory of criminality. Garaudy points out that ". . . the existentialism of Sartre has been in some manner 'historicized.' "[14] Garaudy also points out the importance of *Saint Genêt: Comédien et Martyr,* in Sartre's development.[15] In this book, published in 1952, Sartre offers the following:

(1). Genet's criminality seems to be related by Sartre to bourgeois society. Sartre writes: ". . . the monster was fabricated in the country, within a traditionalist and archaic culture, and his strange religion reflects the 'primitive' mentality of property owners."[16]

(2). Genet, Sartre writes, ". . . has no *history.* Or, if he does have one, it is behind him. In order for a man to have a history, he must evolve, the course of the world must change him in changing itself, and he must change in changing the world, his life must depend on everything and on himself alone. . . ."[17] But although Sartre here conceives of history as "chance events," or as daily life, he adds: ". . . we cannot exist in any time for ourselves as a totality. Genet is a totality for himself. . . . [N]othing can act upon him from without. His only purpose, his only chance of salvation, is to act upon himself on the level of reflection, so as to accept unreservedly, with love, the horrible destiny in store for him."[18]

(3). Possibly it even may be said that Sartre condemns Genet for failure to realize his humanity through and by means of historical necessity. Perhaps this may be called Genet's bad faith. As Genet is dominated not by history, but by theory and practice of eternal return, Genet, Sartre writes, is

> entirely taken up with reliving ceremoniously his original crisis, concerned solely with repeating and imitating the archetypal gestures of others, disdainful of profane time and deigning to know only the sacred time of eternal recurrence, this adolescent is not *historical.* He refuses irreversibility, change, the new: he has become a rigorously constructed and almost autonomous system that turns round and round and that is self-operating. . . . [T]he sequence of his states, the succession of his feelings and acts of will, is *circular.*[19]

Elsewhere in this book Sartre says:

> The myth of Eternal Recurrence is not in the least bit evident, and Nietzsche never bothered to furnish proof of it.[20] [Sartre here confronts Jaspers, who writes that Nietzsche's idea of eternal recurrence is philosophically as essential as it is questionable.][21]

If Sartre's considerations regarding Nietzschean eternal recurrence were united with deepened thought relating to the unhistorical, abstract theory of ideal types developed by Neo-Kantianism, especially by Dilthey and Max Weber, it would affect not only the theory of types of crime, but also threaten the general validity of certain American sociology. Sartre seems to be condemning not only Nietzschean type-theory of eternal return, but also Heidegger's conception of history developed in *Sein und Zeit*.[22]

(4). Although Sartre may not be aware of the legal conception of infamy, he in effect offers an idealist, existentialist presentation of that alienating institution, developed out of his theory of the role of the stare or look:

> For right-thinking people, Genet embodies the Other. And as he has fallen into their trap, he embodies the Other in his own eyes too. But this Other, who has been installed within him by a decree of society, is at first a *collective representation,* of which it has all the characteristics. Fixed and intangible, it cannot be reduced to the contingent movements of an individual consciousness. It is Genet himself, but *with another nature.*[23]

In a subtle development which cannot be set forth here, Sartre recounts in effect how Genet, through solipsism, alienates the infamy-alienation, appropriates the appropriation involved in loss of civic fame. "For the solipsist and for Genet," Sartre writes, "*I is Another,* and this Other is God."[24] Genet's solipsistic and mystical alienation of infamy-alienation may be contrasted with Hegel's theory of the responsibility of the criminal to win his freedom through the necessity of the criminal law. It should also be compared with first, the Marxist theory of the role of *praxis* (work) in achieving historical freedom through and within historical necessity, and second, with the Marxist theory of the aid of other men in realizing such achievement. In forcing attention to the sanction of infamy-alienation (for which Bentham perhaps gives scores of synonyms in English), Sartre is emphasizing the importance of this punishment in the criminal law.

Infamy is a criminal sanction which the Fifth Amendment reserves to the people by requiring grand jury indictment and petit jury conviction for a formulated crime. But what has developed in the United States since World War II has been the infliction of infamy by the executive or by committees of the legislature (for instance, by the House Un-American Activities Committee) in violation of the Fifth Amendment. The Supreme Court has sought to blunt some qualities of governmental infamy. Nevertheless, except for Justice Douglas and perhaps for Chief Justice Warren, the Court has not acknowledged that there is such a conception as infamy. The Court is not willing to recognize that the Bill of Rights has other than English common law antecedents. The concept of infamy is not an Anglo-American concept, but developed in ancient and feudal Roman law. It is related to the theory of excommunication. The attack on state-imposed, anti-democratic infamy summed up in the Fifth Amendment derives not from English feudal law, but from the French Enlightenment and its condemnation of feudal alienation.

The Supreme Court has not been aided in understanding the Fifth Amendment by American legal scholarship, which is committed to the theory that the Bill of Rights is exclusively of English origin. These jurists are unwilling to conceive the possibility that there was an American Enlightenment which received certain of the thought of the French Enlightenment. They will not explore this possibility because it may lead to the conclusion that the American Revolution was a social revolution and not merely a national liberation movement.

References

1. FRANKLIN, M.: The significance of stoicism in Roman law in the development and outcome of Hegel's theory of alienation. *Acta Juridica*, 1958, p. 250.
2. HEGEL, G. W. F.: *Lectures on the History of Philosophy,* trans. by E. S. Haldane. London; Kegan Paul, Trench, Trübner and Co., 1892, pp. 440-443.
3. SÈVE, L.: Sur la conception marxiste de la responsibilité. *La Pensée,* nouvelle serie, n° 101, p. 99.
4. HEGEL, G. W. F.: *The Phenomenology of Mind,* 2nd ed. trans. by J. B. Baillie. New York; Macmillan, 1931, p. 236.

5. SHARGORODSKII, M. D.: The causes and prevention of crime. *Soviet Sociology, 3*:27, 1964.
6. LEKSCHAS, J. and HARTMANN, R.: Basic problems of socialist criminology. *Law and Legislation in the German Democratic Republic,* 1966, Nr. 1, pp. 17-19.
7. RENNEBERG J., and KRUTZCH, W.: Social foundations and forms of organization of the fight for the gradual suppression of criminality in the G D R. *op. cit.* 1966, Nr. 1, p. 5.
8. FRIEDRICH, C. J.; The power of negation: Hegel's dialectic and totalitarian ideology. In Travis, D. C. (Ed.): *A Hegel Symposium,* Austin, U. of Texas, 1962, p. 34.
9. POUND, R.: *Outlines of Lectures on Jurisprudence,* 5th ed., Cambridge, Harvard U. P. 1943, p. 60.
10. REICHENBACH, H.: *Modern Philosophy of Science.* London, Routledge and Kegan Paul, 1959, pp. 73-74.
11. BERNAL, J. D.: *Science in History.* New York, Cameron Associates, 1954, vol. 2, p. 532.
12. MARGENAU, H.: Meaning and scientific status of causality. *Philosophy of Science,* 1934, vol. 1, p. 148.
13. RECK, A. J.: The philosophy of Brand Blanshard. *Tulane Studies in Philosophy, 13*:146, 1964.
14. GARAUDY, R.: *Perspectives de l'homme.* Paris, Presses universitaires de France, 1959, p. 107.
15. *Ibid.,* p. 105.
16. SARTRE, J.: *Saint Genet, Actor and Martyr,* trans. by Frechtman. New York, New American Lib. 1964, p. 359.
17. *Ibid.,* p. 339.
18. *Loc. cit.*
19. *Ibid.,* p. 358.
20. *Ibid.,* p. 378.
21. JASPERS, K.: *Nietzsche,* trans. by C. F. Wallraff and F. J. Schmitz. Tucson, U. of Ariz., 1965, p. 352.
22. HEIDEGGER, M.: *Being and Time,* trans. by John Macquarrie and Edward Robinson. New York, Harper, 1962, pp. 424-55.
23. Sartre, *op. cit.,* p. 162.
24. *Ibid.,* p. 163.

INDEX

147